）

*f*P

Will You Take Me As I Am

JONI MITCHELL'S *BLUE* PERIOD

Michelle Mercer

FREE PRESS

New York   London   Toronto   Sydney

FREE PRESS
A Division of Simon & Schuster, Inc.
1230 Avenue of the Americas
New York, NY 10020

First Free Press hardcover edition April 2009

FREE PRESS and colophon are trademarks of
Simon & Schuster, Inc.

Permissions acknowledgments appear on page 228.

For information about special discounts for bulk purchases,
please contact Simon & Schuster Special Sales at
1-866-506-1949 or business@simonandschuster.com.

The Simon & Schuster Speakers Bureau can bring authors
to your live event. For more information or to book an event
contact the Simon & Schuster Speakers Bureau at
1-866-248-3049 or visit our website at www.simonspeakers.com.

Designed by Suet Yee Chong

Manufactured in the United States of America

10   9   8   7   6   5   4   3   2   1

Library of Congress Cataloging-in-Publication Data
    Mercer, Michelle.
        Will you take me as I am : Joni Mitchell's Blue period / Michelle Mercer.
            p. cm.
        Includes bibliographical references and index.
        1. Mitchell, Joni. Blue. 2. Mitchell, Joni. I. Title.
    ML410.M6823M47 2009
        782.42164092—dc22   2008050426
    ISBN-13: 978-1-4165-5929-0
    ISBN-10:   1-4165-5929-9

For my common and illuminated one

And they said to him, "But play, you must,
A tune beyond us, yet ourselves,

A tune upon the blue guitar,
Of things exactly as they are."

—WALLACE STEVENS,
"THE MAN WITH THE BLUE
GUITAR"

Contents

A Note from the Author

Unless cited in the notes section or attributed to other sources in the text, quotations are from my original interviews.

Will You Take Me As I Am

Introduction

You've probably known this kind of girl. Maybe you've been her. I certainly was, at eighteen.

When a guy seemed like a decent prospect, there was one good way to find out. A true test of character. An absolute gauge of worth.

"There's something I want you to listen to," I'd say.

The CD cover alone suggested a drama of introspection. It featured her downcast face, the eyes half-closed, the high sculpted cheekbones of a fairy queen, all withdrawn in a wash of blue. Not any kind of blue. Not sky blue or cornflower blue or turquoise, the manufactured shades of crayons, makeup, tulips. This blue was an experiential palette, a product of living. The shadow in the spotlight. Smoke's invitingly acrid edge. The ocean at dusk after you've been swimming in it.

You didn't play Joni Mitchell for girlfriends. At least I

didn't. I already knew they got it. She clarified murky emotions so you could immerse yourself in them. The conflicting need for love and independence was less troubling when expressed with such vividness and precision, and feeling that comfortable with ambivalence was like being able to breathe underwater. I wanted to lie next to someone who experienced the same ravishment of self-reflection when he listened, and until that happened I could dream. So I played the record alone, ruminatively, or for a potential lover, expectantly.

The guy usually intuited that Joni appreciation was a kind of foreplay.

"That's good," he'd say.

It was tough to muster a response equal to that sound, especially in the era of ironic grunge and cold cynicism in pop music, of "here we are now, entertain us."

"But do you hear the lyrics?" I'd ask. "I mean, are you really listening?"

The boy might produce an insight about the poetry of a song. Something along the lines of "I like the idea of drinking a case of somebody." But even such an ace response wasn't enough. My strict religious upbringing regarding sex had relaxed into a kind of chivalric code wherein virtue, while no longer sacrosanct, was still nonetheless a rare treasure of which someone must prove himself worthy. There was yet one more test.

"How do you like the music?" I'd ask.

Meaning: can we disappear together to another time and

place? A soul mate would hear the ingenuity of Joni's chords, the novelty of her song structure. Could he see blue sounds and feel chords as colors that can be imaginatively strummed or alternately tuned into mutant shades? Was the combined power of her words and music animating new reaches in him?

The guy might quite reasonably decide I just wasn't worth it. In 1990, Tori Amos die-hards were less trouble, as they required something less than a shared religious experience. Still, a strong few soldiered on, willfully misreading my anxiety as sexual desire. Joni's songs "had their own moods," they'd say, or make some other adequate observation. A reference to Chopin would have been better. And just one comparison of *Blue* to Debussy's work would have been best of all.

"The people who get the most out of my music see themselves in it," Joni Mitchell told me. I was roughly the eighty-nine millionth teenage girl to have an existential transformation through *Blue*, though I can't be sure how many went on to use it, like me, as a litmus test for sensitive boys. *Blue* redefined autobiographical songwriting so it seems only natural to begin discussing it with something of a diary entry. Please, however, don't hold my memories against the record or Joni. She's already taken enough blame for being a muse to every flaxen-haired girl who picked up a guitar and mistook emotional turbulence for art.

As long as I'm being honest, you should also know that I

went on to reject *Blue* in favor of Joni's more obscure and challenging work with jazz musicians, and moved on to test men with albums like Joni's *Mingus* and *Don Juan's Reckless Daughter* or John Coltrane's *A Love Supreme*. Gradually, Joni became for me an exemplar of a woman who could hold her own in the man's world of jazz. But studies have shown that the music we meet at our most self-involved, in adolescence, is the music that hits us deepest. For me and tens of thousands of other teenagers, that music was from Joni's autobiographical period, or what I like to call her Blue Period, which began with *Blue* in 1971 and lasted through 1976 when she made *Hejira*. Between those recordings came *For the Roses*, *Court and Spark*, and *The Hissing of Summer Lawns*, which were more or less personal, too. Listeners who know these albums tend to know every lyric and note.

I first spoke to Joni in 2004 for my Wayne Shorter biography. Joni adores Wayne. He has played soprano saxophone on most of Joni's recordings since 1977. She calls him "the only genius I've ever worked with." Knowing she'd be reluctant to talk with a writer, Wayne called her with this testimonial: "Michelle's originally from Kansas, but she clicked her heels three times and ended up in Oz with me." That was intriguing enough for Joni to call me—eventually, at the eleventh hour, when the book was near completion—and offer up insightful descriptions of Wayne's "pictorial" playing and stories of his musical superhero feats in Japan and around the world. "It's nice to talk to someone about Wayne and jazz," she told me then. "The work of mine that everyone disparages rather than the earlier stuff that's gotten recognition and locks me into the suffering singer-songwriter image." Mitchell is ambivalent about her legacy as a singer-songwriter and defensive about her status as an autobiographical artist.

This past summer Joni screened a film of her 2007 ballet, *The Fiddle and the Drum,* for a small group of us at an outdoor amphitheater on British Columbia's Sunshine Coast. It was a magical night, watching the film under the stars, surrounded by orange-barked arbutus and giant lodgepole pine trees. Joni called the occasion "Ballet in the Bush," and was clearly thrilled to be showing such rarefied art in what is still essentially a fishing community. Keyed up like a teenager, she drank white wine from the bottle, watching the film intently and moving along to the music, shadowing the dancers' movements.

"See, don't I deserve more than one gear in my career?" she asked me afterward.

As the ballet shows, her career, after having powered through many gears, is now in overdrive. In the decades after her Blue Period, Joni reinvented herself as a jazz artist and as a lyricist of social critique as well as of self-disclosure. Part of what so excites Joni about her ballet is having a more accessible setting for her less renowned songs from the 1980s and beyond. "It's really exciting how broadly it communicates all these difficult and obscure songs. The fact that they were never appreciated sticks in my craw. I thought, *I've got to somehow popularize this before I die.* My songs have long soliloquies, like Shakespeare. They need action to sustain the interest of some people. The ballet gives them that."

When it comes to her celebrated earlier autobiographical songwriting, Mitchell's a little like a beauty queen who seized the crown in the swimsuit competition—when she feels like she actually deserved to win for personality, talent, and her bright response on how to achieve world peace.

> "It's been a little frustrating that everything was compared unfavorably to *Blue*. They wanted me to stay in that tortured way. I peeled myself down to the bone, there was no place left to go. I had to start building up and healing myself and looking outward. You know what I mean? You start with yourself, then you extend yourself to your family, you extend yourself to your community, then you extend yourself to the world—depending how much energy you have."

Mitchell doesn't want to be reduced to autobiography as she feels it celebrates her early, first-person work to the exclusion of her later music, in which she undertook social commentary, and projects like the ballet. Besides, even in her highly autobiographical period, she assumed other characters and personae in the hope that people might identify closely with them.

"The beauty as a listener is you have an option. Either you can see yourself and your humanity in the songs, which is what I'm trying to do for listeners. Or you can say, 'That's the way she is' and equate the songs with me. The richest way, the way to get the most out of it, is to see yourself in it. The ones that do, whether they call it autobiographical or not, are getting it."

She believes such identification is impossible if a song is too closely connected to her own experience. But I think part of the reason people see themselves in Mitchell's work is because she put so much of herself on the line. And identifying with her music does not exclude wondering about where it came from and just what she risked in making it.

Joni also resents being reduced to a musical memoirist because it puts the art behind the feeling, when in her work feeling is a construct of art. She sees herself as a playwright or storyteller presenting characters and scenes that dramatize emotions and experiences—experiences that may or may not be her own. The fact that Mitchell portrayed herself as an untutored musician and unschooled poet has promoted the view of her as an artist who instinctively lays out feelings on record. But as a look at her dense lyricism and strange guitar tunings shows, *Blue*'s intimacy is matched by its esthetic rigor: Mitchell tore her heart out and put it on tape as masterfully as it's possible to do. In *The Wounded Surgeon*, Adam Kirsch discusses the major confessional poets in ways that can also illuminate Joni's work. Confession is a "bad metaphor for what the most gifted of these poets were doing," Kirsch writes, because their "primary motive was aesthetic." He performs a rescue-and-recovery project for Robert Lowell, Elizabeth Bishop, John Berryman, Randall Jarrell, Delmore Schwartz, and Sylvia Plath, investigating their major techniques and themes and showing how they transform the messy disorder of life into art.

Like the so-called confessional poets, Joni had to cultivate some exceptional strengths and skills to create the "art songs," as she calls them, of her Blue Period. In assessing that art, it seems necessary to look at another vital issue. After recording *Blue*, she suffered a crisis of self-exposure and retreated to British Columbia for about a year, where she built what would become her summer cottage. This hermitage had always intrigued me, and it proved even more fascinating after Joni and some of her close friends told me exactly how much she changed in this time away. Once back in Los Angeles, she turned to jazz just as personal songwriting was being popularized and taking a turn for the worse. The final aspect of her Blue Period, which I discuss in the last chapter, was a rather supernatural meeting with a Tibetan lama who helped Joni find a gentler approach to self-scrutiny. That came through on *Hejira*, Mitchell's 1976 autobiographical masterpiece, which I present here as a bookend to *Blue*.

*   *   *

Joni is very open to artistic inspiration, always fooling around with language, riffing on ideas and images, casting about for the *mot juste*, the deft turn of phrase. Art for art's sake is very much at play in her conversation. At times it seems as if every other line is a metaphor. Discussing her distaste for jazz that loses sight of the melody, Joni said, "With the old jazz standards they'd state the melody in the first verse, and then they'd start to deviate; they'd do the courtesy of a point of departure. With this deconstructivism, they just tear the song all apart and never put it back together again. It's like a watch with all the springs on the table and you can't tell what time it is."

It would be natural to equate Joni with the somber, self-scrutinizing persona of her songs. But in truth, she's a lot more fun than that, as one of her oldest friends, Tony Simon, affirmed. "Inside it all, she is such a fun-loving, happy person with a sense of humor. She gets serious about things she believes in sometimes, but the fact is underneath all of that there's a fun-loving streak in there that's wonderful. And if you said, 'We're going to a party, you know, and not sure who's gonna be there, but we want to raise some hell here,' she's the best person to go with."

When I first interviewed Joni for my Wayne Shorter biography, she talked a blue streak on just about everything, delivering bright lines of poetry and complete paragraphs of philosophy. I heard little of the bitter and humorless grouch I'd often read about in the press. She was a gregarious, clear-eyed observer of modern culture and a great storyteller. Joni's reputation for seriousness may have something to do with the scope of her vision and the loftiness of her expectations. For example, Joni told me that while she appreciates Coltrane's innovation, she ultimately considers his music "overrated" and "neurotic." I suggested he didn't live long enough to mature fully, to move beyond preaching his own neuroses in music. "Exactly," she said, warming to the topic. "Since the churches have failed, it's the artists' duty more than ever to admire the Dickenses and the Kiplings and the Beethovens and . . . to not settle, not to be jumping three feet and think you're jumping six foot eight." I wouldn't put Dickens in the same category as Beethoven, but I admire her drive toward excellence and the idiosyncrasy of her great man canon, despite the seeming arrogance of her standards.

This exaggeratedly solemn reputation is also in part the result of her music being used so widely as therapy. In her songs, listeners often hear their deepest feelings articulated for the first time. Epiphanies of that magnitude don't leave much room for humor. Creating those moments of epiphany takes vision and perspective. "I'm not an uncheerful person," she once said. "The melodies I love have a wide emotional spectrum; you have to be quite cheerful to face these themes." Even the songs from Mitchell's Blue Period have plenty of humor and wit. She has a huge capacity for silliness. One time we were talking about her Buddhist practice. "I guess I'm a half-assed Buddhist as long as I'm an artist," she said. "You're still tapping into your passions to bring it back into the art."

I disagreed and said, "I think the art is the other half of the ass."

"Which end is it?" she joked. "It's not like I'm holding up the rear."

Considering Joni's humor, storytelling, and utter transparency in life and art, her Greta Garbo mystique just doesn't hold up. On one subject, though, Joni has remained very mysterious and guarded: her romantic life. Her enduring defensiveness on the topic stems from the period when *Blue* was recorded. In 1971, *Rolling Stone* printed a chart of her romantic conquests, including Graham Nash, James Taylor, and Jackson Browne, dubbing her "Old Lady of the Year," and even worse, "Queen of El Lay." Joni had split with Graham Nash in 1970 and taken her damaged heart to Europe, where she wrote some sad songs, most likely for Nash, and some love songs, most likely for James Taylor, whom she also started dating that year. You hear all that on *Blue*. But Joni doesn't reveal any specific sources for the songs, again for the reason that fixed detail denies listeners the freedom to insert their own experience into her lyrics. Such gossip detracts from the most powerful listening experience, the personal one.

That doesn't stop fans and journalists from analyzing her songs as romans à clef, decoding key metaphors to declare one lover or another the definite subject of a lyric. Taylor was recently asked about the origin of "River," a song he now performs. "River" is most likely autobiographical, Taylor allowed, given that "it starts with a girl from Canada watching them try to make Christmas on La Brea in Los Angeles." He declined, however, to interpret the lyrics any further: "Do I want to know who she made cry, who she made say good-bye? Well, I haven't asked her that question. That's the only mystery in it: Who was it whose heart she broke?" With a laugh, he added, "There were a lot of us."

Celebrity gossip is not very compelling to me. It seems based on the notion that details of celebrity lives are inherently more interesting than those of our own. Paradoxically, it's also motivated by a desire to bring celebrities down to our own level. Luckily, the art of songwriters is even more fascinating than their love lives. They have inspiration and talent that the rest of us don't. And if Joni is playful with her muse, she's obsessive and meticulous about how she transforms that muse into art. This book is my old-fashioned appreciation of that process, as well as an effort to say something about the literary nature of songwriting. I have so much gratitude for these songs that I want to better understand how and where and why they were made, and in sharing my understanding perhaps enrich the songs' value in the culture. So when I discuss Mitchell's relationships with James Taylor or Leonard Cohen, it's primarily to trace influences and find connections among their styles and strategies. Basically, I'm more interested in how songwriters make their work personal than in what they get personal about.

Joni Mitchell is an artist about whom fans will always say, "You don't know her like I do." Her work can touch you so deeply that it's hard to believe yours is not a unique experience. For that reason, her work invites zealotry and esoteric interpretation, the stuff of a mystical order. Woe befell the adolescent acquaintance of mine who suggested Joni and Rickie Lee Jones were "pretty much the same," and that guy at the party who remembered her as "the one who slept with all the guys who sang 'Woodstock,' right?" Actually, Mr. Room Temperature IQ, she *wrote* "Woodstock." My holy war was on.

Over the years, I calmed down enough to attempt the objective work of a music critic and came to accept there's simply no accounting for taste. Still, when Mitchell began receiving awards in the mid-'90s, it seemed to me the honors missed the mark quite extravagantly. Mitchell would arrive at ceremonies in a haze of old-school glamour, in luxurious folds of fabric and jewels, exuding the holy smog of her American Spirit cigarettes. The award granters usually wore an air of self-congratulation, pleased to have occasioned another coronation graced by the queen of pop herself. But the presenters' grandiloquent generalizations about Mitchell as "one of the greatest living songwriters" didn't often say much about her actual talents and gifts.

Accepting the trophies, Mitchell showed more bemusement than gratitude. "They were giving me awards, but they didn't know why," she told me. "A lot of my art and the nuances of it were never recognized." Joni admits she has a big chip on her shoulder, though I understand where she's coming from. No written appreciation of Mitchell's work has ever gotten at the depth and texture of the feelings her music provokes in me. I hope her fans will also want to know more about why they are so moved by the hybrid force of her words and music. There was great artistry involved and much emotional truth at stake when Joni asked, "Will you take me as I am?"

1

In the Manner of the Ancients

THE SPRING OF 1970 WAS A LITTLE LATE FOR
Joni Mitchell to be dropping in on Matala. In 1968,
Life magazine had printed a lavishly illustrated
seven-page cover story on the town's flourishing
expatriate hippie culture. In a rocky beach cove just
outside the village of about seventy-five people, *Life*
reported, America's disaffected youth was taking
up residence in a merry beehive of cliff caves. The
freckled and wholesome Rick Heckler and Cathy
Goldman, a kind of countercultural Adam and
Eve, adorned the cover: "Young American nomads

abroad, two Californians at home in a cave in Matala, Crete."
Some of the kids were "merely off on a lark, doing what the
young have done for generations," sympathized *Life* writer
Thomas Thompson. But there were "too many others caught
up in some sort of aimless journey toward an unknown destination." Even Ulysses, who was fabled to have stopped off at
Matala, had been trying to get home. This self-indulgent generation, the writer's tone suggested, was rejecting everything
his readers had struggled to build. These kids were running off
to live in caves after all.

But a lot had changed in the two years since the Matala
cave colony received such prominent mainstream coverage. By
the time Mitchell arrived, parents were not shocked so much as
disappointed when their promising college graduate children
eschewed gainful employment for a rocky cave somewhere in
Greece. Some of those parents were even beginning to work a
Matala hippie tour into their sightseeing swings through the
islands. Enterprising Greek villagers had put up a concrete
parking lot in the muddy town square for the tourists.

If you had to arrive after they paved paradise, it was even
more unfashionable to come as Joni Mitchell did, in pleated
pants, looking like the successful California recording artist she was. It was pretty fancy attire for a place where kids
would drive fifty miles to sell their blood for 350 drachma at
the Iráklion hospital. Of course, some of those kids were only
playing at poverty; others would be living with it more permanently. The appeal of Matala was that these two kinds of

cave dwellers—the middle-class dropouts and the poor kids—could enjoy the same low-rent, high-principled existence there. Idealism was the great leveler.

In talking to some of the people who were in Matala at the time, I discovered something about the culture of the place. On the island back then, cave dwellers loved to talk about Matala's history, bypassing America's recent troubled past for nostalgic refuge in the birthplace of Western civilization. Hippies would refer with equal credulity and confidence to the myth that Ulysses himself had stopped there and the fact that the caves had been cut into the accommodating sandstone in Neolithic times. The ancients had used the caves as burial sites, someone had heard. Pirates stored their spoils there. At one time it was a leper colony. The point was, the cave dwellers were the latest in a long lineage of outcasts and freaks, the kind of people who make their own way. The sheer yellow-gray cliff reaching out like a long cradling arm into the Mediterranean was a visual reminder that hippies had come there to "put out," as the New Testament said metaphorically, "into deep water." That water as seen from the caves was emerald or sapphire or turquoise, depending on the day or who was looking. Always a rich, jewel-toned hue—in the cave dwellers' estimation, it was such an elemental place that the water seemed to be its own reward.

In the caves, last names had as little meaning as time. One guy went by Proteus. Another was known as Yogi Joe. In spite of her striking Scandinavian beauty—infinite blond hair, tall, lean frame—and fine, well-pressed clothes, the practice of

dressing for a trip a holdover from her small-town Saskatchewan youth, Mitchell arrived pretty anonymously too. Most
of the cave dwellers had been checked out of the culture since
Joni had achieved some success. Just that month Mitchell had
received a Grammy for "Best Folk Performance" for her album
Clouds. Even back in the United States, many people didn't
know she was the one who'd written their generational anthem, "Woodstock," capturing in it the alluring prelapsarian
notion of getting "back to the garden." Crosby, Stills and
Nash sang and owned the song just as various other performers were largely credited with Mitchell's other popular songs:
Tom Rush for "Urge for Going," Buffy Sainte-Marie for "The
Circle Game," and Judy Collins for "Both Sides, Now." It would
be a couple of years before Joni Mitchell posters would grace
thousands of dorm room walls.

Mitchell was hoping to blend in with the crowd. She was
looking for an escape, as well as a little fun. She was in crisis.
In January, she had announced a break from touring, canceling
appearances at Carnegie and Constitution halls. She played a
final show at Royal Festival Hall in London and returned home
to finish *Ladies of the Canyon.* She thought she'd retreat in Laurel Canyon, her leafy eucalyptus haven rising into the hillside,
home to her friends, who happened to be some of rock's strongest talents, including her lover Graham Nash.

"I was being isolated, starting to feel like a bird in a gilded
cage," she told *Rolling Stone* reporter Larry LeBlanc later that
year at the Mariposa Festival, after she had returned from her

travels. "I wasn't getting a chance to meet people. A certain amount of success cuts you off in a lot of ways. You can't move freely. I like to live, be on the streets, to be in a crowd and moving freely." Already, some of her best music had been stimulated by travel. A clarinetist whom she saw playing on a London street inspired "For Free." "Big Yellow Taxi," which along with "The Circle Game" was the closest she had ever come to a sing-along hit, was composed when she was on vacation in Hawaii and looked out her hotel window to see a parking lot in paradise. Life in the studio and on tour could become self-referential, and Mitchell was keen to escape the industry for a while. "The experiences I was having were so related to my work. It was reflected in the music," she said. "I thought I'd like to write on other themes. In order to do this, I had to have other experiences." She wanted to become her own muse again. Travel would force her to greet each day, person, and scene with a fresh perspective.

There were other reasons Mitchell wished she "had a river to skate away on," as she sang in "River," a song she'd written that winter. She couldn't shake her reputation as an angelic folksinger, which had plagued her ever since *Rolling Stone* had called her the "penny yellow blonde with a vanilla voice" upon her recording debut in 1968. Also annoying was the constant confusion with Joan Baez and Judy Collins, which had something do with the similarity of their names, true, but Mitchell also saw it as proof that no one was interested in hearing the growing musical complexity that distinguished her from those folk maidens. Worse, her record label, Reprise Records, was making it its business to sell her as a countercultural mascot. Upon the release of *Ladies of the Canyon*, Reprise took out an advertorial in *Rolling Stone* with a fictional story about a very hip chick—the sort who tie-dyes curtains for her Volkswagen van—who's been through a bad breakup but finds solace in the combination of a strong joint and Mitchell's new record. No hippie Madonna, Mitchell needed a break from her own love life: her life with Graham Nash had certainly seemed idyllic in his 1969 song "Our House," but she had turned down Graham's marriage proposal, realizing she couldn't settle down with him. Maybe she'd find out exactly why on the road.

Mitchell did have one standout hippie prop on hand in Matala. A few months earlier, she had commissioned a mountain dulcimer from a local Los Angeles artisan, Joellen Lapidus, and she took her new instrument on the road. The dulcimer's soft but bright drone served Mitchell well in the nightly cave music circles, where she held it across her lap, strumming melodies with a flat pick and sliding depressions of the strings to create her own accompaniment while she sang. There was no room for dancing in the caves, so Yogi Joe performed hand dances that cast surreal shadows on the cave walls.

In Matala, Mitchell sometimes borrowed a Gibson guitar from Johnny McKenzie. When he played his songs for her, he remembers her commenting that David Crosby would have liked them. They'd hike together through the fields, looking at peasants walking donkeys in the rustic countryside. Johnny told Mitchell he'd chased a woman across Europe and was sad because he knew she'd never belong to him. "If you want that girl," he also remembers her saying, "give her a baby." He's glad he didn't do that, no matter how heartbroken he was then.

By mid-April, five weeks into her stay, Mitchell—along with the promise of free food—was the main draw of a highly anticipated event advertised as the "Matala Hippie Convention," which worried the local Cretan authorities. But pretty much just the same old cave crowd showed up to hear Mitchell sing Bob Dylan's "Mr. Tambourine Man," a tune she'd never consent to do back home. By then she was ready to go. When you're running away it's easy to run in the wrong direction. Matala was the kind of place where you went to get free but ended up a prisoner in something like Plato's cave allegory. Ensconced in the countercultural lifestyle, the shapes of the outside world began to appear less real than hand shadows on the cave walls. Back in 1968, when the *Life* magazine reporter had relayed the news of Bobby Kennedy's death and met with no reaction, let alone the stunned grief he expected, he asked, "Is this the new phenomenon? Running away from America and running away from emotion?" "Back to the Garden" had bucolic overtones. But back to the caves? "Everybody was getting a little crazy there," Mitchell said. "Everybody was getting more and more into open nudity. They were really going back to the caveman. They were wearing little loincloths."

It didn't look like the free-spirited vagabond role suited her any better than those of iconic folk maiden or someone's old lady. She'd have to keep trying to get out from under the myths that other people imposed on her—and that she sometimes imposed on herself. Mitchell knew the caves' communal life was too distracting for an artist. Now, work would come more easily away from Crete, back in the city. As Annie Dillard wrote, sometimes artists need a room with no view, a place where imagination can meet memory in the dark.

Mitchell arrived late to Matala but left just in time. As Johnny McKenzie remembers it, that was "just after the tourists climbed down the one-bucket well" to bathe, and "just before electricity came." Often on trips to Crete, the Greek island shuttle boat seemed as if it would sink in the sea's huge waves. McKenzie and Joni took the same boat on the return trip, and he says the Mediterranean was so calm that it reflected Mitchell's face like a mirror. After so many salt baths, she was looking scruffy enough to resemble the hippie Madonna she was reputed to be.

But Mitchell's listeners already know this. Or at least have sensed it. The hippie travel, the escape from the bonds of marriage, the grand dance between romance and disillusionment, the emerging realization that one's true motives and feelings are not as pure as hoped. We know what she was fighting and seeking as she left Matala and headed to maybe Amsterdam, or maybe Rome, where she'd rent a grand piano and put some flowers round her room. It's there in the confidences and professions of her music.

"*Blue* is partly a diary," Joni told me. "It's me moving through the backdrop of our changing times. I was in Matala and we got beach tar on our feet and then I went to Ibiza and

I went to a party down a red dirt road, then I went to Paris where it was too old and cold and everything was done. But it's also more than a diary. It's one chapter in the Great American Novel of my work."

THE SOUND OF "ALL I WANT" is earthy, strong, and high-toned, attuned to a Mediterranean landscape. You might think you hear a rhythm section. It's actually just Mitchell alone, slapping her dulcimer's strings in a calypso beat while a drone adds a tinge of contemplation. After a few bars of these rhythm chords, she brings in some harmony at an odd interval, a fourth, its sense of suspension heightened by the dulcimer's thin tone. The music moves in a headlong rush, on an exuberant, high-strung search for something.

When Mitchell begins singing, the music has already conveyed mood so vividly that even the simplest lyrics register great poetic impact.

> *I am on a lonely road and I am traveling,*
> *traveling, traveling, traveling*
> *Looking for something, what can it be?*

Lyrics and music are so intricately combined that listening is a pleasant confusion of word and sound. The splitting open of self in the lyrics is like a minor chord with no possibility or need of resolution. This is an aural postcard from the edge of feeling, and its intensity is expressed in odd intervals, rhythmic energy, and the strangely thin over-strummed timbre of the dulcimer.

Even back in 1970, smoking has already thickened Mitchell's vocal cords and brought her upper range down from the helium highs of earlier records like *Clouds*. But the awareness of her own imperfection gives her voice new grit and backbone: even up high she can no longer be mistaken for Snow White singing to birds, as was sometimes the case on her earlier folk-inflected records.

James Taylor joins in on guitar, mellowing and warming the tune. He plays chords, mostly, momentarily breaking those chords into chains of notes that relax the music and add a little leaf and vine to the landscape. Taylor and Mitchell were in love when the recording was made, but this is tempered by Mitchell's lyrical admission that love can be tainted by other emotions.

> *Oh I hate you some, I hate you some, I love you*
> *some*
> *Oh I love you when I forget about me.*

Along with its spare arrangement, this animate truth makes "All I Want" as affecting now as it was when first released in 1971. Above all, there's more raw emotion and nerve than anything Mitchell had done before. "I was demanding of myself a greater and greater honesty," she said of the period in which she recorded the song in a 2003 PBS interview, "so that it strikes against the very nerves of people's lives." Like the other songs she wrote in 1970 and recorded on *Blue*, "All I Want" has the sound of dawning self-knowledge. The music has shades of an intensely interior existence confronting the big sky and open water of experience. Because that's how Joni Mitchell's life played out that year. Mitchell went out traveling to find herself and is telling us what she found. Just after the record was finished, she played it for some songwriter friends.

"At that time we were still young enough that we played our songs for each other. It horrified all the male singer-songwriters around me. I was amazed. They'd listen to it and they'd go [*swallowing sound*]. They were embarrassed for me. Because the popular song had been about posturing. It had been self-aggrandizing. The feminine appetite for intimacy is stronger than it is in men. So my songwriter friends listened and they all shut down, even Neil Young. The only one who spoke up was Kris Kristofferson. 'Jesus, Joni,' he said. 'Save something for yourself.'"

ZEUS WAS BORN twelve miles north of Matala and about several hundred miles south of the place he proclaimed the center of the earth: Delphi, where heaven and earth met, where man was closest to the gods. In Delphi, the oracle received the god Apollo's first commandment: "Know thyself." This notion of the self as the passageway of spiritual ascent was so central to the Greek worldview that Apollo's directive was inscribed over the oracle's doorway.

Knowing yourself is one thing. Writing, or singing, or even just revealing that self-knowledge to others is another. How did we get from knowing yourself to baring yourself so nakedly that people recommend that you just clam up? For that, we have to look away from Delphi, south of Matala, as Mitchell did when she sang, "The wind is in from Africa / Last night I couldn't sleep." As a resident of the seaside cliff caves, you heard and felt the *sorokos* howling from the Sahara, carrying scorched dust or the rough dream-robbing phantom of it, all the way from Libya. While Mitchell's self-observation stems from ancient Greece, the fact that she told us about her sleeplessness—her very act of letting us in on it—can be traced back across the Mediterranean to the North Africa of the fourth century. There was of course an intervening millennium or so and lots of significant literary and social history around the world. But essentially, it all goes back to Tagaste, near ancient Carthage, where St. Augustine of Hippo was born. It was Augustine who first defined and exemplified the practice of revealing the self and its history in words, thereby inventing autobiography in the Western world.

In 397, when Augustine began to write the thirteen books of his *Confessions*, he had been a baptized Catholic for ten years and a bishop for two. Ordination sat rather uneasily with Augustine. He wanted a monastic life rather than his bishop's church service job, which carried a magistrate's tedious responsibilities. By training, he was a rhetorician, the late Roman period's equivalent of a man of letters, but that's not why he wrote the *Confessions*. He addresses that issue, for God and for us, at the beginning of Book 1. "Why then do I put before you in order the stories of so many things?" Well, it's because he's lost. "I have become an enigma to myself," he says, "and herein lies my sickness and inner struggle." Since his own questing mind is his closest companion, Augustine has the bright idea of using that mind to objectify and understand himself. In merging Augustine the protagonist and Augustine the narrator, he will come to know himself.

In the *Confessions*, we learn that the thirteen-year-old Augustine stole from a pear tree not for the gluttony of savoring the fruit but for the pure evil thrill of the theft; after he made off with the pears, he'd throw them to the hogs. He never mastered Greek, for which he blamed a brutal teacher who constantly beat his students. He had a child with a concubine whom he loved deeply but would not marry because of the social and political consequences. He also felt guilty about his continuing attraction to a mystical brew of Manichean philosophy and astrology.

As Patricia Hampl discussed in her introduction to Augustine's work, what he confesses is not nearly as important as how he does it. When he began writing, Augustine intended his work to be read or recited communally, as was customary in this period before publication was invented. Then one day he had an epiphany when he came upon his mentor, Ambrose of Milan, reading alone silently to himself. This unusual sight changed his methodology of writing and his approach to the word itself. To accommodate the solitude of a lone reader, focusing oneself on one text, Augustine crafted a narrative that clearly and closely illuminated the workings of his own mind. "The *Confessions* is startling because Augustine has found a way to reveal the profound intimacy of a mind thinking," Hampl wrote. "This is the narrative engine that drives autobiography: consciousness, not experience, is the galvanizing core of a personal story." It is a mind in pursuit of meaning that we encounter for the first time in the *Confessions*, the desire to understand and the admission of what he does not: "These writings are not true confessions of mine," he writes, "unless I confess to you, 'I do not know.'"

The *Confessions* are not truly an autobiography, though— the first genuine autobiography was written 1,300 years later by Rousseau. Augustine's confessions are a collection of those fundamental life episodes in which he can find and promote the inexplicable actions of God's grace. The word "confess" has double meaning here. First, it is an inventory of one's thoughts and actions, which for Augustine means a confession of sins. But he is also confessing the truth he knows about God. To confess is to glorify God through an act of humility because after confession God can grant or deny salvation.

Having laid his own soul bare and concluding his personal history at the end of Book IX, Augustine then feels justified in proclaiming the origin and meaning of good and evil for everyone. In Books XII and XIII, Augustine fixes his attention on the first chapter of Genesis, performing a verse-by-verse exegesis in which he holds Adam and Eve responsible for everything: "The deliberate sin of the first man is the cause of original sin." Therefore, he asserts, everyone must be baptized and confess one's sins to cleanse oneself of them, just as Augustine himself has done.

The cost of Augustine's great literary leap, then, the price of his innovation of first putting consciousness onto the page, is shame. Something of the mystical Augustine does live on in certain often-quoted phrases: "Our whole business therefore in this life is to restore the health of the eye of the heart whereby God may be seen." But Augustine the mystic was no match for Augustine the architect of sin and salvation. "The confession of evil works is the first beginning of good works," he also wrote, much more influentially. After Augustine's *Confessions*, there was no closeness to God without the soul-cleansing redemption of owning up to sin. He made shame the only route to holiness.

JONI MITCHELL HATES ST. AUGUSTINE and loves to vent her antagonism in stories about him. As Vic Garbarini wrote, Mitchell is a "great storyteller in the ancient Greek tradition, not so much describing or analyzing a situation as conjuring up landscapes of cinematic power that take the listener vicariously through the event. You emerge from the other side with the feeling that you've lived the event yourself and maybe even learned a lesson or two." Indignation raises the stakes in her stories. Disbelief yields colorful details, outrage evokes sharper, more clearly defined characters, and derision stimulates a heightened sense of action. Mitchell blames Augustine for much that is wrongheaded in the Judeo-Christian tradition. By her account, he misattributed his own human failing of cowardice (not marrying the woman he loved) to original sin, and then had the chutzpah to turn the faulty notion of original sin into doctrine. Sure, Augustine finished off mysticism as a legitimate route to the Christian God, but her real grievance with him is that he's a "champion bullshitter"—that is, he regimented the act of confessing the truth and made it dogma without seeking the deeper truth about himself and his own messy motivations. He didn't know himself well enough to serve the inner reality of the human condition, which is what Mitchell believes anyone who puts pen to paper should do—and what she's striven to do throughout her life's work. Mitchell is nevertheless seduced by these moments in his narrative that are surrounded by a magical aura. Conversion moments make for good stories. As Mitchell sees it:

> "Augustine was in love or in lust—in his opinion, he was in lust—but he was attached to a woman with whom he had a child. They were unmarried, but that was okay, the times were very liberal. But he was expected to marry above his station, rise into the court. He had risen very high because

he was a silver-tongued devil, but the next political move was to marry a rich woman and move up the political ladder, which was acceptable back then. But he couldn't let go of this woman with no money.

"The Bible hadn't been formulated yet, but Augustine had the letters of the Romans, in some form or another. He'd been reading them and he was abandoning Virgil and Cicero in favor of Luke. He was out in the backyard sweating all this out, this impossible situation: he couldn't let go of this woman; he was screwed because he couldn't just dump her. Through a synchronistic event, he heard a girl, a child skipping in the neighboring yard. This book I was reading said, 'In the manner of the ancients'—this synchronicity was something that people valued back then. Of course, it's still alive and well today, at least in the arts community. So in the manner of the ancients he heard this child skipping, and the skipping rhyme he heard was saying, 'Pick it up and read, pick it up and read.' And he went in and opened the book of Romans and he came across this passage that was really hostile to lust.

"He adapted that stance and that formed this crazy interpretation of Genesis. Which is such a chopped-up story anyway. Huge sections of it cut out Lilith, for example. Among other things. Like the two trees. The Tree of Knowledge gets all the attention, but there's also the Tree of Everlasting Life in it.

"Well, I've got my own idea of that story, of what a better interpretation of that story might be, a better interpretation of it than a man who's upset because he can't let a woman go and marry another woman to progress his career. To think about the influence that he's had on the world because of his own obsessions . . ."

AUGUSTINE'S WORK BENEFITED from a transitional period in Christian history when an ironclad doctrine was just what the Church wanted. With their enormous social upheaval, the 1960s were also a prime time for a talented Holy Roller or despot—or songwriter—to glorify a personal obsession into a powerful cult, dictatorship or tune. Lo and behold, Bob Dylan wrote the song "I Dreamed I Saw St. Augustine," in which he heard the saint sounding his "sad complaint" in a voice "without restraint." This dreamy evocation of Augustine was really nothing more than one of Dylan's personal obsessions, but thanks to his mythic vision and bardic voice, "I Dreamed I Saw St. Augustine" became a song of great influence and a testament to Dylan himself. No matter what Dylan wrote about, fans wanted to listen.

And he wrote about whatever pleased him. Mitchell, whose autobiographical accounts have more epiphanies than a James Joyce story collection—more conversion moments than even Augustine's confessions—often cites the transformative effect of first hearing Dylan's "Positively 4th Street" when it was released in 1965. The song is verse upon verse of beguilingly tuneful vitriol directed at someone who betrayed him. "You've got a lot of nerve to say you are my friend / When I was down, you just stood there grinning." The sentiment is personal, and its intention is that the listener take it personally. Never before in songwriting were sore feelings and disdain tossed off in such a disarmingly colloquial style. In Mitchell's telling, she was enlightened the moment she first heard this song; it threw open a hidden door to the self's wide world of subjective topicality. "Oh my God," she said to herself then, as she later recalled, "you can write about anything in songs!" And eventually she would. Of course, what Mitchell wrote with this carte blanche was quite different from Dylan's songwriting—as distinct as sadness and anger, as the colors blue and red.

What unites Bob and Joni, the royalty of songwriting, is their common starting point: they both came of age in folk music's pop heyday. They broke away from the folk tradition with as much inevitability as the so-called confessional poets broke away from modernist dicta in the 1950s. Not that the folk world had so well wrought a doctrine as poetry, whose modernist figurehead and spokesman, T. S. Eliot, both showed in verse and told in criticism. It was one thing when Eliot's masterpiece *The Waste Land* demonstrated the high art of symbolism; it was another when his critical essay "Tradition and the Individual Talent" explicitly dictated the ideal tone of a poem as impersonal and crafted to perfection, with no concern for the figure of the poet himself. Eliot's allusive, symbolic, and, yes, impersonal style reigned supreme when confessional poets came of age—and it was that style which Robert Lowell left behind when he wrote the confessional verse of *Life Studies*, that Berryman took issue with in *Dream Songs*, and Elizabeth Bishop moved beyond in *North & South*.

Folk music's hero was, of course, Woody Guthrie. Guthrie led by example, not by precepts, although his charisma and songwriting skills gave him a certain messianic quality. Most poets engaged and argued with Eliot, even as they toed his line; musicians simply followed Guthrie. He was a journeyman, traveling across the United States to learn traditional folk and blues songs, trailing migrant workers from Oklahoma to California. Guthrie's observations of the economic and environmental hardships of the Dust Bowl era inspired him to write his own lyrics about working people, which he set to traditional folk music. Topical songwriting as defined by Guthrie meant chronicling a plane crash of migrant workers soon after it happened, with politics giving the lament implicit meaning. "I am out to sing the songs that make you take pride in yourself and in your work," said Guthrie—a goal that would impact his most popular song, "This Land Is Your Land," a response to Irving Berlin's "God Bless America." Guthrie's original 1944 version contained two recriminatory verses, but he later killed them to preserve the wholly patriotic tone of the version that went on to become an American songbook classic. His songs told the truth—as long as it was an uplifting truth.

In the late 1950s, growing pools of folksingers in Cambridge and Greenwich Village took Guthrie's lead and focused on the issues of the day, especially civil rights. Though all these musicians knew and admired Guthrie, the one to seek him out in his declining years at the Greystone Hospital in Morristown, New Jersey, was Bob Dylan. Dylan idolized Guthrie, calling him "the true voice of the American Spirit"—indeed, Guthrie is one of the few subjects Dylan does not obfuscate in his memoir *Chronicles*. When Dylan first hit the coffeehouse scene in New York in 1961, he could be accurately introduced onstage as a "young folksinger" who "sang a lot of Woody's tunes." In those days, a musician was presented with a body of songs, or "rebel ballads," as Dylan liked to call them, so authoritative that it took real ingenuity even to think beyond them. Within a year or so, though, Dylan began to have some doubts about the populist style of topical songwriting, with its focus on real events: "You could usually find some kind of point of view in it and take it for what it was worth," he writes in *Chronicles*. But "the writer doesn't have to be accurate, could tell you anything and you're going to believe it." Those rousing, heartfelt folk songs didn't always offer much opportunity to find or tell inner truths.

A larger cultural shift was coming. The conformity of the 1950s was giving way to the 1960s ethos of individual freedom, and this epochal shift would also change Dylan's approach to songwriting. Some of the 1960s ideals borrowed from the Enlightenment period of the French Revolution, which also sought to invent a new culture of man. Jean-Jacques Rousseau, an important Enlightenment figure, was also the originator of the modern autobiography.

Augustine had established the conventions for writing a confession, conventions that St. Teresa of Avila and many others had observed in their autobiographies. But while the motives for these confessions were theological, Rousseau would reclaim both the act of confessing and the early title *Confessions* for his own purposes. "By Rousseau's age," notes *Confessions* translator J. M. Cohen, "men had begun to see themselves not as atoms in society that stretched down from God to the world of nature but as unique individuals, important in their own right." Rousseau's soul baring is a matter of principle, but it's not a Christian principle, and his commitment to honesty initiated the Romantic practice of analyzing the self as an end unto itself.

The soul-baring ideal thrived in the '60s, and helped Dylan, who like Rousseau had an almost religious sense of self-importance, break through folk music's conventions with songs like "Positively 4th Street." Dylan's later shift from acoustic to electric guitar scandalized the folk establishment, but that was just a change in external form. More radical was his departure from the political advocacy of Woody Guthrie–style folk in order to sing songs of himself. The Canadian folk scene from which Mitchell first emerged was defined less by political songwriting than by the broadside balladry of the British Isles, though that left just as little room for personal subjectivity in lyrics. She needed to hear Dylan. After Dylan had transitioned from social commentary and folk storytelling to his personal song-poetry, Mitchell also moved to more autobiographical material in 1970 on *Ladies of the Canyon*. She confessed ambivalence over commercial work, comparing herself unfavorably to a noble sidewalk musician in "For Free." She shared her deep feelings for Graham Nash in "Willy": "I feel like I'm just being born / Like a shiny light breaking in a storm / There are so many reasons why I love him."

And then she went even deeper on *Blue*. But while bitterness offered Dylan some self-protection, Mitchell's *Blue* songs were stories of self from a time when she had no defenses at all. "My individual psychological descent coincided with my ascent into the public eye," she has said. "They put me on a pedestal and I was wobbling. I thought I'd show them who they were worshiping." Mitchell often says she found her poetic ideal in the words of Nietzsche's Zarathustra, who envisions "a new breed of poet, a penitent of spirit; they write in their own blood." Joni was entirely a creature of her feelings, and in this way was like Rousseau, who explained their primacy in his *Confessions:* "I have freely told the good and the bad, and have hid nothing wicked, added nothing good; and if I have happened to make use of an insignificant ornament, 'twas only to fill a void occasioned by a short memory." An accurate memory was unimportant to Rousseau because his *Confessions* were the fruit of faithful attention to his emotions. He was sickly throughout his life and hypochondriac besides, always preoccupied with sensations of comfort or discomfort. His pleasant, calm, or violent attitudes toward other people and himself were as changeable as the weather—which also affected him deeply. He revels in feelings as his inner truth, and that inner truth is what he aims to share in the *Confessions*. "I may omit or transpose facts, or make mistakes in dates," Rousseau writes at the start of his seventh book. "But I cannot go wrong about what I felt, or about what my feelings have led me to do; and they are the subject of my story." This fidelity to human truth is the legacy that Rousseau handed down in Western culture, which eventually made its way into the culture of autobiographical songwriting.

Mitchell's originality as a songwriter was not to write music about just anything—Bob Dylan had already done that—but to investigate her inner life and make its inchoate aspects concrete in lyrics and music, to excavate and flesh out her feelings. "The writing has been an exercise in trying to work my way towards clarity," she said in the 2003 PBS interview. "Get out the pen and try to face the beast yourself. And what's bothering you, right? Well, that's not exactly it. It's very hard peeling the layers off your own onion. When you get to the truth, do I want to say that in public?"

IN AUGUST 1970, Mitchell was forced to figure out just what she was willing to reveal in a very public moment. The third and final edition of the Isle of Wight Festival took place on East Afton Farm in Freshwater, England, and its bucolic setting put attendees in mind of Woodstock. But the crowd grew unruly as promoters tried to keep out people who hadn't paid by putting up corrugated iron fences and hiring police to patrol with trained guard dogs. When things got ugly during Mitchell's set, she confronted the audience.

The mood of Mitchell's performance at Isle of Wight was a preview of the *Blue* album, which she was then writing and would record a few months later. On the festival stage, she came off as kind of angry, kind of vulnerable, kind of sad, but with a cold blue steel will to tell the crowd exactly how she felt. One night at dinner, I asked her how she managed to gather up her courage at Isle of Wight. Almost forty years later, it's still one of her favorite stories:

"The first time I stood my ground was there, in front of half a million people. It was a hostile audience. Some French rowdies stirred people up, based on the fact that we had sold out because we arrived in fancy cars. Neil Young and I rented a red Rolls. It was decadent backstage. So there was an 'us versus them' mentality from the audience, we performers were seen as privileged and elite, putting on royal airs.

"Some acts canceled and there was a gaping space in the program. For about an hour, no one would go on. So it created a dead space. I was scared witless, but wanted to be cooperative. I said I'd go out. Onstage I had a broad perspective on the crowd and its energy that you couldn't see from inside it. Soon after I started—maybe in the second song—a guy near the front started flipping out on acid. He let out a banshee yell, like he had the devil at his heels. The whole crowd started undulating with waves of his energy. It was not good. There was brewing unrest.

"I moved over to the piano to play 'Woodstock,' which was kind of funny—this event was more like a war zone than Woodstock. A guy from the caves, Yogi Joe, who taught me my first yoga lesson, he suddenly appears on the stage. He gave me the victory sign and says, 'Spirit of Matala, Joni!' And then he starts playing congas— with terrible time, the time of a disturbed child. I bent over to him and told him it was entirely inappropriate. At the end of the song, Yogi Joe leaps up and grabs the mic: 'It's desolation row and we're all headed to hell!' or something like that. The guards grab him. The crowd had already been agitated, but this really riles them up: 'They've got one of ours!' and they're moving forward.

"I wanted to run, but I'd been running away a lot, canceling shows, you know, to travel and avoid the big stage. But here's where I got my strength. With Dennis Wilson and James Taylor, I'd just been at a Hopi ceremony, a snake dance ceremony to bring rain to their corn crops. They dance with live snakes. One stood up on its tail and rocketed into the audience. The people parted like the red sea, but the musicians, who were priests, these drummers, kept playing, kept the groove. They knew they had to bring the rain."

Videos of Mitchell's Isle of Wight set tell the rest of the story. Unsure what to do about the crowd, she bought time by vamping on a piano intro to "My Old Man." She was the very image of feminine vulnerability in a long yellow dress and a turquoise belt and bracelet she'd just bought at the Hopi reservation. After a couple minutes of holding back tears, her chin quivering with the strain of it, her confusion hardened into righteous indignation. She stopped playing and addressed the crowd.

"Listen a minute, will ya? Will ya listen a minute? Now listen . . . A lot of people who get up here and sing, I know it's fun, ya know, it's a lot of fun. It's fun for me, I get my feelings off through my music, but listen . . . You got your life wrapped up in it and it's very difficult to come up here and lay something down when people . . . It's like last Sunday I went to a Hopi ceremonial dance in the desert and there were a lot of people there and there were tourists . . . and there were tourists who were getting into it like Indians and there were Indians who were getting into it like tourists, and I think that you're acting like tourists, man. Give us some respect."

"And the beast lay down," Mitchell said, finishing the story. "The beast lay down. Depending on who you asked, I either saved the festival or was the victim of it." Concertgoers have mentioned that Mitchell couldn't see or hear the noisy helicopter that flew overhead during her set—the real object of the crowd's jeering hostility. Regardless, it was good practice for her: even while keyed up in the face of a large, restive crowd, she could stand her ground by speaking with intimacy and honesty. She finished out the show with several more songs, including "A Case of You" and "California," which would appear on *Blue*.

"NO, NO, NO, NO!" Mitchell yelled, pounding the table with her cigarette-free hand. We were outside smoking after dinner, during which she had told her Isle of Wight story. I had remarked that Joni's obituaries might very well focus in on this period in the '70s when, as she said onstage at the Isle of Wight, her "life was wrapped up" in her music, when she brought new literacy to personal songwriting. I had suggested that, like it or not, her most enduring legacy might even be as a "confessional songwriter." Never one to mince words, Mitchell said, "That's as close as someone could come to calling me a nigger." She went on to say:

"When I think of confession, two things come to mind.
The swinging light and the billy club, you know, trying

to get a confession out of somebody that's been captured. Confess, confess! Or a witch hunt. Or trials. Confession is somebody trying to beat something out of you externally. You're imprisoned. You're captured. They're trying to get you to admit something. To humiliate and degrade yourself and put yourself in a bad position. Then there's the voluntary confession of Catholicism. Where you go to this window and you talk to this priest and you tell him that you're having sexual fantasies and he's wanking on the other side of the window. Both of those things, that's confession. That's the only two kinds of confession I know— voluntary and under duress—and I *am not* confessing.

Graham Nash told me much the same thing: "I think the word *confessional* has a religious connotation that I shy away from and so do most of my friends. So I think that that is the problem with confession. It implies guilt and something that you did wrong. And none of that is true."

My first experience with confession came during second grade, at my Catholic grade school, when we were excused from math class and marched single file to the church next door. One by one, we were ushered into the curtained booth. I eavesdropped on my classmates' confessions. Debbie Mays had stolen candy? Really? On the other hand, it came as no surprise that Brian Lee had hit his little brother.

When it was my turn, I recited, "Bless me, Father, for I have sinned. This is my first confession." I was burning to get to the freshly memorized Act of Contrition prayer, where I knew I'd shine. But first, I was asked by Father Mohr to unburden my seven-year-old soul of its many sins. I couldn't come up with any.

"Have you stolen?" he asked.

No.

"Well, did you cheat in school?"

No.

"Did you get jealous of your sister or brother?"

No.

"Did you help your mother as much as you could have?"

I sensed Father Mohr's growing impatience as he moved down his list in order of decreasing gravity, from sins of commission to sins of omission. Back in 1980, when the culture of therapy hadn't yet softened the church, and secrets were too terrible to meet face-to-face, our small-town Kansas church still practiced anonymous confession. But through the plastic haze of a book-sized window I could make out Father Mohr's aged profile, visualize his bulbous red nose. I'd been so pleased when he'd sat down across from me in the school lunchroom that day and had stifled my nausea when he'd accidentally spit some spinach into my milk—a priest wasn't supposed to make you sick to your stomach. He'd recently been at the family farm, a holy star in our midst, to help us dig up potatoes in the garden (consecrating both priest and potatoes in my mother's mind) and to talk baseball with my dad out in the milk barn.

Sitting in the dark, draped confessional, I wanted so badly to appease Father Mohr with an overripe peccadillo, rich in horrible detail. Some spoiled and rotten deed that he could sink his teeth into, something he could present to God in exchange for the clean bill of forgiveness he would then fetch back for me from on high. While I worried about how grievous a sin it might be to concoct one, Father Mohr waited in silence, an old hand at this kneeling booth show. Finally, the time-honored process of extracting confessions joined forces with my eagerness to please. I committed my original sin right there in the confessional booth: I told the priest a lie by telling him I had lied.

Artists who commit themselves to the autobiographical form, revealing their thoughts and feelings in song or verse or prose, sometimes place themselves in a position similar to mine in the booth. They are required to cough up juicy admissions and pretty lies because the form demands it. What Mitchell and so many others disdain about being thrown into the confessional category is partly its implication of an original or basic flaw as the starting point for a poem or song. The term connotes a need to flush out and thereby cure what isn't actually in need of revealing or healing and perhaps may not even be there at all. Sylvia Plath condemned the idea of poetry as "some kind of therapeutic public purge or excretion."

But artists' common contempt for the "confessional" tag is about something even more crucial. Elizabeth Bishop lamented the trend toward "more and more anguish and less and less poetry." Pain alone is no credential for a poet. Poetry is not merely recorded experience—maybe painful, maybe not—but experience transformed into insight by invention and expression. Or as Mitchell says, "Sometimes you write about the exact thing you saw, but other times you take something that happened over here and put it with something over there." The difference between mere disclosure and the enduring work of Bob Dylan, Joni Mitchell, or Robert Lowell is at once simple and profound. Mitchell identifies that difference as art.

"Art is artifice and it doesn't matter whose life I scraped to get that text. Of course, I have more access to my own. If you spend a lot of time alone, that's your major resource—your own experience. If I have a human revelation about myself, that's the kind of thing that inspires me to say, 'There is a human element worthy of a song.' It doesn't have to be very big. You can make a good play out of anything, including yourself. But songs traditionally didn't carry these literary elements, and that's what my contribution to the songwriting form probably was, to bring songs closer to something like a good play. But I'm not making these songs out of a need to confess to anyone; it's out of a need to create a story. It works in plays; it works in movies. 'I could have been a contender . . .' Was Brando confessing? People get Academy Awards for that kind of stuff and they don't call them confessional."

For the most part, Mitchell's claim seems accurate. The confessional literary innovation of Augustine was the basis for autobiography, which was in turn the basis for personal songwriting. Yet "confession" is the wrong word for what Mitchell does. She doesn't strive to tell the truth about herself. She strives to find and express human truths, and in the process, she happens to reveal quite a bit about herself. "In songs I'm developing characters and experiences which may or may not be based on myself," she said. During the first half of the 1970s, Mitchell's songs were often based on her own experiences. "Yes," Joni went on, "my songs have always been more autobiographical than most people's." So while her Blue Period may not have been confessional, it was about as personal as songwriting had ever been.

2

Eyes on the Land and the Sky

IN EARLY MARCH OF 1967, JONI MITCHELL
was on a short break from gigs at folk clubs, somewhere between Toronto's Riverboat and Philadel-
phia's Second Fret. She was reading Saul Bellow's
Henderson the Rain King. She remembers being on a
plane. Near the beginning of Bellow's novel, Henderson flies to Africa. The bird's-eye view moves
him to say that in an age when people can look up
and down at clouds, they shouldn't be afraid to die.
Mitchell "got hung up on the passage"—she never
finished the book—and quickly wrote "Both Sides,

Now," performing the song onstage just a few days later. Unlike most of Mitchell's music, the song was fairly standard, written in major keys, with few harmonic pinwheels. This musical repetition had a purpose: her static fix on the same harmonic paths captured a basic mood of disillusionment. Meanwhile, the song's lyrics broadened verse by verse, first looking at clouds "from both sides," one naïve and the other worldly, then considering love and finally all of life "that way."

An elegiac tone, a soft-focus philosophy, and a tune as pretty as a swan made "Both Sides, Now" an instant standard, first recorded by Judy Collins and eventually by 595 other singers and counting, everyone from Frank Sinatra to Dengue Fever. Mitchell's own version appeared on her 1969 album *Clouds*. "I took a lot of flack for recording 'Both Sides, Now' because I was very young," she told me. "A lot of people said, 'What do you know about life?' Some people deemed it kind of pretentious for a twenty-something, who looked like a fourteen-year-old, to stand up and say 'I've looked at both sides now.'" Her authority to look back ruminatively at the ashes of a ruined past was indeed a little shaky. Though she had faced the traumatic decision and rather adult choice of whether or not to give up a daughter for adoption (which she ended up doing), she was young enough still to be in search of settings and experiences, moorings to which she might attach the song's air of loss and nostalgia.

Besides an innate gift for metaphor, there's another good reason Mitchell might have been able to look at clouds—and, by extension, at love and life—from both sides at the tender age of twenty-two. She grew up in Saskatchewan, above the forty-ninth parallel where the flat land and big sky can encourage and even require its residents to take a broad view. Long before Joni Mitchell wrote "Both Sides, Now," Saskatchewan's wide-open spaces had acquainted her with the loaded, metaphorical nature of the sky and the clouds. Some of Mitchell's earliest landscapes were those that engulfed the village of Maidstone, Saskatchewan, where there was nothing to break up the vast expanse of sky. By the time she moved to the city of Saskatoon at age eleven, her perspective was set. "We used to spend a lot of time on the riverbank," Mitchell's childhood friend Sharolyn Dickson, another Saskatoon resident, told me. "I remember us going down there and laying back and looking at the clouds and figuring out what we could see in them."

Over the years, Mitchell has quite publicly celebrated her prairie heritage. At Saskatchewan's Centennial in 2005, she was the local girl made good. "Saskatchewan is in my veins, that stark beauty and the smell of it, the sages and so on," she said. "I'm a flatlander, period." That same year she released *Songs of a Prairie Girl,* for which she rounded up all her songs with lyrical references to home. There were too many for one CD. Like early American folksingers, Mitchell has long used natural images to set a mood for a song ("I was standing on a noisy corner," in the song "For Free"; "The wind is in from Africa," from "Carey"). It has frequently been observed that Canadian culture has been shaped by the experience of the country's geography and natural world; landscapes have been a prime subject of both Canadian painting and poetry. Margaret Atwood, who received a star on Canada's Walk of Fame on the same day Mitchell did, said, "One of the primary interests for a Canadian writer always has to be geology followed by geography." Even an urbanite Canadian like the Montreal-raised Leonard Cohen had enough of the frontier in his songs to make them a suitable soundtrack for Robert Altman's existential western, *McCabe & Mrs. Miller.*

Mitchell also often focuses on landscape in her visual art, which is full of Canadiana in general. The orange-red prairie lily, Saskatchewan's provincial flower, brightens many of her paintings. In the self-portrait on the cover of *Clouds*, she seductively holds a garish prairie lily; the Saskatchewan River runs behind her, ominous yellow clouds and the Bessborough Hotel on its far shore. In other works, she has superimposed photos of native landscapes onto self-portraits. There's a collapse of self into land when she makes a wheat field of her face, for example, an intimacy to the point of merging with the land. The traditional background landscape comes to the foreground in the space the person usually occupies in self-portraiture. When foreground and background share a single plane like this, the meaning is clear: the land is a part of her. Where does it end and she begin?

There's an intimacy with landscape in Mitchell's music, too, and it is certainly a resonant part of the self-disclosure in her autobiographical Blue Period. From the beginning of her career, reviews have made reference to the midwestern, prairie texture of her music, though the meaning of this vague description is not self-evident. Mitchell hears it, too, more specifically in the pulse of her songs. "I've always thought Neil [Young] and I have carried a loping prairie walk in our music, a loping pulse," she told me. "As opposed to reggae, which for me has a tree frog sound. The sound of frogs chirping in the Jamaican trees rises to the upbeat, like the music. Nature is always there in the sound of music, and in mine it's the prairie, where I'm from."

But the prairie in Mitchell's music, or any music for that matter, is more elusive than it appears in her lyrics or paintings. Music and landscape both move us deeply in ways we don't always understand. Landscape architect Frederick Law Olmsted, who most famously designed Central Park in New York City, said landscape was a lot like music—both are nonverbal forms of communication that affect us subconsciously and profoundly. Olmsted would sit inside the Grand Canyon, for example, and ask himself not just how the environment was beautiful, but how it made him feel. How might he try to give other people this feeling, too, even in the city? Lots of great musicians think the same way: What is the shape of my experience now, and how can I translate that into musical form, so listeners can feel it, too?

The terms "landscape" and "soundscape" come up so frequently in music criticism that one of my newspaper editors banned them from his arts section. But it's natural to think of music in terms of architecture. Listening can be a three-dimensional experience, at least. Anyone who's heard music stoned knows that the act of listening can feel like sculpting spaces out of the air. I remember the first time I drove under the influence of strong pot, playing a CD of Charles Mingus's *Ah Um*, and had the visceral sense of being on a musical avenue, with the horns lining it like trees and his bass parading down it like a badass marching band. I have to describe this sensation with images in order to get it across, though it wasn't something I *saw*. I wasn't hallucinating. It was something I felt—and continue to feel in music, even now, when I'm never stoned.

Classical composers have long loved to embody the natural world in their music. Kids in music classes are told to listen for the instrumental characters in Prokofiev's *Peter and the Wolf*: the bird's theme is played by a flute, the cat's by a clarinet, the wolf's by French horns. Vivaldi's most widely beloved work is *The Four Seasons*, early program music with accessible picturesque effects—the violin in the "Winter" concerto evokes swirling snow, for instance. Vivaldi wrote sonnets related to each concerto, with elements of a scene-packed adventure allegory: barking dogs, crying shepherds, storms, children ice-skating, and burning fires. The natural scenes of *The Four Seasons* are those of stylized musical theater set in a mannered palazzo garden.

Mitchell has a special affection for the small group of what she calls "pictorial" composers, and includes herself among them. "This is where we get into Debussy-land," she says. "With *La Mer* you see the ocean, you see the butterflies. Mozart was very mathematic, you know, the agility is amazing, but it's not very metaphorical. Not very many people can paint pictures with notes. Wayne Shorter and I are both metaphorical musicians, and so is Debussy and so was Beethoven sometimes." Beethoven had such extraordinary ears for natural sounds that he continued to compose them into his work after he went deaf and could no longer hear them. The natural touchstones of his Sixth Symphony, the *Pastorale*, are spelled out in his movement titles: Awakening of cheerful feelings upon arrival in the country, Scene by the brook, Happy gathering of country folk, Storm, Shepherd's song; cheerful and thankful feelings after the storm. "Scene by the brook" starts with a 12/8 meter that sounds like the passing of water in a stream. Still, Beethoven said his Sixth Symphony is "a matter more of feeling than of painting in sounds," and its music doesn't strive to conjure mental pictures so much as call up the mellow, spine-pulsing sensation of sitting streamside on a warm afternoon, among many other experiences.

But the flatland of Canada or America is not a site of respite from the city, like Vivaldi's picture-book garden, or even Beethoven's wilder, farther-flung countryside that cheers one "upon arrival from the city." The flatland is all encompassing, all there is. Growing up on a Kansas farm, I was twenty-two before I realized Andrew Wyeth's *Christina's World* depicted a paralyzed woman's struggle through the grasses. To me it seemed a very thin girl was simply enjoying a sprawling refuge on a plain while looking back at her home, which didn't look all that great compared to the flowing grass in which she sat. The world of the grass was rich in all the possibilities of self; the house was circumscribed, someone else's old news. I had to be instructed to see the painting's perspective: home was the destination and some pathology must be coming between Christina and the domestic comfort she sought. Seeing a painting's intended point of view requires at least a little distance between subject and object. When self and land are fused, this distance is gone and perspective is accordingly skewed or crushed altogether.

The way a composer experiences nature can be heard in his music. When someone from the Canadian flatlands, like Joni Mitchell or Neil Young, puts native landscape into music, it doesn't come out like it does in the music of Beethoven or Vivaldi. Flatlanders' early perceptions of landscape are not set so far apart from themselves. So landscape in the music of Young and Mitchell is at once more subtle and manifest, because their feelings for the land have a sound less distinguishable from their feeling of the land itself.

JONI MITCHELL WAS BORN in Alberta and raised in Southern Saskatchewan, the only two land-locked provinces in Canada.

Saskatchewan produces more than half of Canada's wheat. To the north there's some wilderness—pine forests, frigid air, and swamps, or muskeg, as they're called up there. Many terms that distinguish Canadian English identify landscape features: the muskeg of the hinterland, the chutes, or saults, of the rivers, the parklands of the prairies, and the bluffs, or stands of trees, on the flat prairie. An occasional island of trees was as much as Mitchell could hope to find at the southern end of the province. When she was a girl—and still known as Roberta Joan Anderson—Saskatchewan was bulking up its rapeseed, or canola, cultivation, but the brilliant yellow canola patches were still unusual enough to seem like apparitions. Most of the immediate surroundings were plowed brown ground or dim yellow-white wheat fields, the transparent blue above it extending into the remote distance.

Joan's father, Bill Anderson, was a Royal Canadian Air Force flyer from Alberta. Her mother, Myrtle "Mickey" McKee, came from Saskatchewan and worked as a teacher in rural schools. As chronicled in Mitchell's musical tribute to her parent's meeting, "The Tea Leaf Prophecy," Myrtle had her tea leaves read in Regina, Saskatchewan, where she was living in 1942, and the leaves prophesied she'd be married in a month. The wartime lack of men of marriageable age made that seem a ludicrous prospect. But soon Bill happened into the bank where Myrtle worked, and after a brief, passionate courtship, they ran off to Moose Jaw, Saskatchewan, for a hurried wedding. Less than a year later, on November 7, 1943, Roberta Joan Anderson was born into her parents' meager wartime life. She looks back on it as a mystical time to have come into the world.

> "The stars do exert an influence. That's part of the wonder of divinity, how accurate they are. And how complex they are. I was born in Fort MacLeod where all of the flyboys were amassing from England and Australia and America to go and fly over to Hitler. At the time I was born that was an energy pocket. The stars were very intense and unusual at that time. There were three grand trines over my birthplace, so that was very unusual and you end up with a lot of gifts."

Down on the ground Joan's influences were more mundane. In 1947, when she was three, the family moved from Fort Mac-Leod, Alberta, to Maidstone, Saskatchewan, where Bill got a job managing the OK Economy store. The Andersons built a humble home at the edge of town on Highway Avenue E, which separated the house from train tracks. The tracks were close enough for Joan to hear the iron heartbeat of pass-ing trains. The sound was like a call to prayer for her: every time, she would run to the living room window to exchange waves with the conductor. The fact that there wasn't much else for Joan to see out there may sound like a cliché, but its effect on someone during these formative years is enormous.

Maidstone's grain elevator scraped at the sky—with all its agricultural trade the village would grow steadily enough that, in 1955, its status was officially changed from village to town. Everything beyond the village was a blank canvas. Farmland slid empty and expressionless into the horizon, with no vanishing point. In such a landscape, one direction is as good as any other, since you have to envision and dream the landscape into being.

The Andersons' move to North Battleford when Joan was six put her on the north bank of the North Saskatchewan River at its junction with the Battleford River, about ninety miles northwest of Saskatoon. "My years there were glorious, really," Mitchell has remembered, focusing back on the experience as clearly as if she were still there. "I loved growing up in Saskatchewan. We always lived on the edge of small towns, so I had the luxury of riding my bicycle into the country, looking for beautiful places, which usually constituted a grove of trees." And if there were even one tree around, she would climb it for a different line of sight on the flat land. Joan stored away these perspectives and feelings as pictorial information first and began to use them in drawings as a child. At a birthday party at age seven, she heard Edith Piaf's "Les Trois Cloches" and asked for piano lessons, but soon quit when she found the piano teacher's instruction too harsh. At nine, Joan saw the Kirk Douglas vehicle *The Story of Three Loves* whose soundtrack included a version of the Rachmaninoff piece "Rhapsody on a Theme of Paganini." The music made her swoon, she remembers, and she'd go down to a department store across from her father's little market, take the record out of its brown sleeve and go into a listening booth to disappear into the music. "You do the bulk of your listening very young," she told me. "And that gives you the mulch out of which your music is going to grow."

In 1953, a polio epidemic struck Canada and Mitchell was unlucky enough to be part of it. She was airlifted to St. Paul's Hospital in Saskatoon, and during the flight, Mitchell looked down to see a small town every few miles. As she wrote in her grade five notebook, from above, these towns looked like "topaz brooches on the black velvet land." Writer Jim Irvin re-tells Mitchell's standard account of her time in the hospital.

"The polio ward of St Paul's Hospital, Saskatoon, was an isolation unit of temporary huts presided over by 'rustling nuns'. Joan's mother would visit wearing a mask to avoid contamination and, on one visit, brought her a Christmas tree. Joan was allowed to sit looking at it twinkling for a while after lights-out. It made her long to go home for Christmas, but the consultant didn't think she'd be well enough, in fact he was unsure she would ever walk again. The disease had twisted her spine forward and to the right. She could hardly stand. There was a regimen of excruciating therapies, including having her legs bound in scalding hot wet rags. Joan bore it all and one day announced she was ready to go home."

Sure enough, she could walk again, and she went home for Christmas.

Joni's self-mythology features polio as the foundational event in her artistic life, the point at which she became an artist. She and others have often portrayed her childhood as Wyeth's *Christina's World* come to life. With nothing but hobbled movement in a sea of grassy desolation, the story goes, she retreated into her imagination and an artist was born. But she'd already shown a talent for art before she contracted polio. Perhaps her childhood in small-town Saskatchewan played as big a part in her origins as an artist as polio did. As an only child, Joni grew up in quiet isolation, believing things were happening to her uniquely, so she attributed unusual significance to her experiences, building meaning from the smallest details and noting patterns in ephemeral events. A single Maidstone United Church wedding she attended with her friend Sharon Bell at age five made such an impression that she would later spin it into the childhood fascination with marriage she portrays in "Song for Sharon." As the writer Flannery O'Connor said, anyone who survives childhood has enough information about life to last the rest of his days.

Mitchell's bout with and recovery from polio did leave her with the sensation of having been to the other side and back: "Polio, in a way, germinated an inner life and a sense of the mystic," she says. "It was mystical to come back from that disease." While it weakened her physical endurance, it also fortified her emotional resolve. Mitchell had the lithe body of a high jumper, and may have been more extroverted and athletic if polio hadn't stolen some of her strength. Mitchell would eventually play the guitar in unique tunings to compensate for the damage polio did to her left hand. Finally, as Mitchell told me, it also made her a provisional churchgoer, which led her to music and gave her new avenues for artistic expression.

"I lost my ability to stand and walk. I made a little prayer saying, 'I'm not a cripple, give me back my legs.' I don't know who I prayed to at that time. I'd broken with the church early. The Bible stories were full of loopholes. I liked the stories, but they didn't like my questions. So I don't know who I prayed to, but I said I'll make it up to you. So I got my legs back and I joined the church choir. Nobody wanted to sing the descant part. I said, 'I'll do it, that's the pretty melody,' the part with odd intervals, fourths and fifths. Most kids couldn't really hear them; they were lucky to hang in with triads."

Besides revealing an early talent for music, this tale of bargaining with the Almighty illustrates Mitchell's drive to express what might not have occurred to other people, and her confidence that she could use her abilities to direct the course of her life. Sometimes artists and their fans try too hard to come up with a source for unusual creativity, even resorting to pathologizing it. A gift for art may be deepened or otherwise influenced by tragedy, but it doesn't necessarily have to be born of it. Maybe Mitchell came into the world as an exceptionally sensitive girl in ways that only nature can explain. Maybe her upbringing on the prairie did the rest.

One night at choir practice, another girl produced some Black Cat cork cigarettes she'd pinched from her mother's purse. Joan joined a group on a frozen fishpond where they lit up the contraband smokes and passed them around. While some of the girls coughed and choked, Mitchell "felt really smart and clear" from her first puff, she told me.

"I've smoked ever since I was nine. In the town where I grew up, kids were really vicious. In order to forget who they were, and who I was, I'd get on my bike and I'd head out to the prairie and watch the birds fly in and out and smoke. When I was fourteen, they sent me to live with my aunt. She said to me, 'You need to smoke this for your nerves. It's good for you. Here's your first ashtray, don't smoke on the street. I'll introduce you to these other women.' They *all* smoked. They all channeled, they all had powers of one kind or another. They were all fine-haired and fine-skinned, too. Like them, I was so sensitive and thin-skinned that my nerves were at the surface. I needed tobacco."

*   *   *

EVERY YEAR IN EARLY SPRING, Joni remembers, she and her best friend Sharolyn would wait for the day the ice broke on the Saskatchewan River. They'd head to the river bluffs after school, looking for signs the big event was coming. Snow and ice slowly melted into the water, which then rose under the surface ice and began to degrade it, helped along by heavier sun exposure from spring's longer days. They watched closely for cracks because once the break started it was over quickly and they didn't want to miss it. When this rite of spring finally came, its violence was mesmerizing, the great plates of splitting ice sounding like rifle shots, or sometimes cannon booms. The broken ice chunks thudded and crashed downstream, pulling along trees torn from the riverbank and whatever else didn't get out of the way. Within a couple of days, the ice would be gone.

The Andersons' final move, when Joan was eleven, took her ninety miles southwest to the relatively lively metropolis of Saskatoon. The town was like many greater cities built on a mighty river, the Saskatchewan, three times as wide as the Seine. Its many bridges earned it the nickname "the Paris of the prairies." The river formed a socioeconomic boundary, separating the staid middle-class east side and more easygoing working-class west side. The University of Saskatchewan brought Saskatoon some arts and culture. More significantly, its considerable distance from any other major city necessitated a cultural scene of its own. Still, bridges aside, it was no Paris: Saskatoon, named after the Cree word for an edible berry, was founded as a proposed capital of a temperance colony. And Joan was still confined by the conservative farming culture that dominated the continent's interior.

Though it was a dramatic change for Joan, there were some advantages to bigger-city life. When she was in sixth grade, a new swimming pool opened just a couple of blocks from her house. She and Sharolyn hung out there all summer, baking their fair skin and swimming, which didn't put too much strain on Joan's scoliosis-beset body. "Esther Williams was kind of our hero at that time," Sharolyn says. "We started emulating her and water ballet—synchronized swimming now—and spent a lot of time in the water. We actually trained to do this water ballet and did a number of performances at the pool's grand opening. And there was a jukebox there inside the pool, and hanging out there was where we all first learned how to dance."

Sharolyn was one of Joan's few girlfriends—she says she's always preferred the company of boys:

"It's the play of boys I understood more than girls. Maybe it goes back to this. My father would come home and say, 'Gee, I had such a good time with the fellas tonight.' My mother would come home and say, 'Those damn women.' Whenever she went out with the Kinettes, she'd come home with her lips pursed and whenever my dad came home from the Kinsmen he'd come home all full of jolly. I think that that gave me the impression that men were fun and women weren't."

Being one of the boys had its challenges. There were dares like crawling across the interior of the Broadway Bridge, an arched bridge that spanned the deep, broad Saskatchewan River from its east to its west bank—and which was also where "Cherokee Louise" hid in the song from Mitchell's *Night Ride Home*. Other tests with the boys were even more risky, like "catching the slow drag," a moving-train maneuver that in Mitchell's description sounds like a scene from a spaghetti western. "You had to climb the ladders of the train and run along the top and then had to go down the ladder and then go all the way up to the front and make a lot of noise so the conductor came back, and then you had to roll out the door. We did some really dangerous things." Joan was frail from her bout with polio but never told anybody: "I just kind of ignored it, which served me well because if I had listened to doctors' orders I wouldn't have had as full a life." The trick was proving herself as a daredevil among the boys without losing her femininity. "If I got too boyish, it would offend them. Suddenly I was behaving like a boy and I was really a girl and they didn't really like that. There were lines—and they were good lines because your own femininity was tied to that."

Mitchell has often credited her poetic awakening to her seventh-grade English teacher at Queen Elizabeth, Mr. Kratzman. He read Rudyard Kipling's *Kim* aloud to her class, and the book gave her a model for male friendships and much more:

> "In a certain way it was very shaping. I identified with Kim, even though he was a boy, because he was an orphan. His nickname was 'Little Friend of All the World.' And the thing that he had as an orphan boy without parental guidance was the ability to skip that training of them and us which the church teaches and parents teach. I'm a mutt. I belong to nothing, and sometimes that's lonely. I don't belong to a school of music. I don't belong to a race. I don't belong to a nation."

Upon learning of Joan's love for painting, Mr. Kratzman told her, "If you can paint with a brush, then you can paint with words."

"It was wonderful of him to bring that out in her but he was tough on her too, because he could see the potential," Sharolyn says. Classmates also recognized that Joan had talent. Her cover design for the grade eight graduation program involved the mortarboarded heads of a girl and boy on a chessboard, implying that they were all graduating onto the chessboard of life. Still, Joan's lack of talent in some subjects infected her with self-doubt. "It's interesting because she doesn't remember being the acknowledged creative meter-stick in elementary school," Sharolyn says. "She doesn't see it that way. We all thought she was in terms of her writing and her art. All the other school subjects were of zero interest to her, and she didn't excel in everything. So she didn't consider herself a complete star. I always thought of her as that."

Joan was certainly no "keener," the then-popular word for a brown-nosing, overly enthusiastic student. "I used to do my book reports off *Reader's Digest Condensed Books*," she told me. "I'm not a bookworm. It's too indoors. I wanted to be out. I wanted to see life. I wanted to experience it firsthand. And I can only remember things that I experience firsthand." The caption for her grade nine yearbook photo at Nutana Collegiate reads, "Her greatest aspiration is to not be a Latin teacher." That year she met Tony Simon, who was the same age but had been skipped ahead to grade eleven. Simon was part of a tight clique of boys who since fourth grade had been in a special, accelerated class for kids with IQs of 130 and above. "We were always 'the boys,'" Simon remembered. "But 'the boys' from grade eleven included Joni. I'm not even sure how you would define that. But it was just, hey, she's one of the boys. There wasn't any secret handshake or anything, but it was how you would talk, what you might say, you know. For her, not a problem." One of Tony's best friends was Bob Mitchell, son of film actor Cameron Mitchell and grandson of Fred Mendel. The richest man in town, Mendel owned Intercon, the intercontinental pork factory, and would go on to found the Mendel Art Gallery. In the late '50s, when Joan and Tony were in high school, "Papa" or "Grandpa" Mendel still combined his business and pleasure, housing a semiprivate art collection above the meat-packing plant. He had parties at which Joan was first exposed to works by Picasso, Matisse, and other European masters.

The following school year Joan moved to the newly opened Aden Bowman Collegiate. She needed a clean start, having developed a reputation for poor attendance at conservative Nutana. Its proximity to downtown was also a problem, since Joan had a habit of slipping over from the "respectable" east side into downtown bars to hear music. "In Saskatoon when we were kids, there was a strong division between the east side and west side," Sharolyn Dickson remembers. "But Joan felt much more at home on the west side. She'd go over there all the time and go to the dances and hang out with people that most would think of as unscrupulous characters. She just loved it there. That was her comfort zone."

Mitchell told me she was content with the music she heard at YMCA dances around town: "As a teenager I was a rock-'n'-roll dancer. So tutti-frutti and sha-na-na-na . . . all of that was fine for me." Elsewhere Mitchell has cast her strong attraction to the "wrong side of the tracks" as the bohemian leanings of a budding musician.

"I gravitated to the best dance halls from the age of twelve to the age of sixteen. Like any young black trumpet player in the South, like John Handy or any New Orleans musician who knew he was a musician at an early age, somehow I was drawn to where the music was best, and it's always in the roughest areas. And yet, the street had heart then, and a child, a baby, a clean-looking baby was not molested. If anything, they were very protective. First of all, they'd say, 'Get her out of here,' or, if I insisted on remaining, they'd make sure that someone saw me safely to the bus."

With her transfer to the new school, Joan didn't have to take the dreaded Latin classes, though she did take French from a popular teacher, Robert Hinitt. Compared to her adventuresome exploits out on the town, her classroom demeanor was resigned. "She was very shy, not pretentious, a modest, gentle girl," Mr. Hinitt remembers. "The kind of girl who never raised her hand in class even when she knew the answer. It's hard to hear her speak now and to realize she was once a very self-effacing creature." Mr. Hinitt also supervised students in the decoration of the gymnasium for the annual graduation dance, and every year they transformed it into another world, a wonderland. Joan's responsibility was painting a huge backdrop mural, and in this endeavor her perfectionism began to emerge. "She would be up and down on a sixteen-foot ladder," Mr. Hinitt said, "so she could see all kinds of things in the painting that she couldn't see when it was flat on the ground." She worked absorbedly on the sets for two months.

While painting and drawing were Mitchell's passion and calling, writing was simply a hobby. In a tongue-in-cheek yearbook report for the writers' club, she put into wry verse the group's loss of its secretary, Larry, who'd "gone to Tech with his talent." She chided "a president who rarely knows when the next meeting is to be held," but affirmed a club project:

We hope to have collected before the end of the year, enough "Quotable efforts" to compile into a book so that everyone in the school may share the "vegetables of our work." (In Writers' Club we are taught not to overwork stereo-typed metaphors. "Fruits of our labor" is so common.)

Many talented sixteen-year-olds are smartasses, but for Joan, scoffing at the rules was no passing adolescent phase. Even back then, memorizing a set of rules was anathema to Mitchell, who was already emerging as an artist in need of finding things out for herself. Mitchell now believes her lyrical ability can be partly attributed to the British literary heritage in Canadian education and is a trait her music shares with Canadian songwriters and performers like Neil Young, the Band, and Gordon Lightfoot. But she's always disdained literary interpretation. "That's one thing I resented about the way poetry was taught in school; this need to pin down its meaning," she said. "I never thought I would become a poet, but when I did and people would ask me to interpret those things . . . If it was only about my experience, how would anybody be able to relate to it? If I tell you more than the poem, then I'm ruining its effectiveness and its value in your life." It benefited Mitchell to dismiss literary diagrams and charts, the rules of metaphor, and standard theories of interpretation. She would go on to be willfully ignorant of the rules of songwriting, and with that freedom would innovate, forging a richly allusive interconnection between melody, harmony, and poetry in her work.

Joan was also "very popular with the boys," Hinitt remembered. "The guys around the foot of this ladder when she was painting, I used to have to fight them off, say 'Get away from Joan, she can't concentrate with you guys.' But she was very popular with the girls, too. I remember she worked at a lady's clothing shop on Saturdays, she wore a red plaid skirt and red sweater and brown and white saddle shoes, and the ankle socks. The other parents used to complain about her beautiful wardrobe, and I used to say she earned all that money herself, so, you know, don't blame me for her clothes. She was very style conscious. Yes, dressed to the nines."

Joan's willowy frame suited clothes so well that she was by default a floor model as well as salesgirl in her after-school and weekend job at Ricki's Ladies Wear Shop. Still, Mitchell was not amused when a well-meaning adult suggested she make a career of beautification. "She came into class one day just crying because Mrs. Sampson, the guidance counselor, told her she should become a hairdresser," Mr. Hinitt remembers. "Poor Joan, she was so upset because she had all these wonderful ideas in the back of her mind." As a teenager, Joan's determination didn't always translate instantly into confidence. But Joan later got her revenge when she parodied a housewife in a piece for the student yearbook:

I am a chronic sufferer of bargainitis—a disease with which every red-blooded female is afflicted . . . For instance last week I bought a brown-shantung dress at Blanche Buchanan's for twenty-eight dollars (a fraction of its former price). At home I surveyed myself before my vanity mirror. "Tres chic," I muttered, although somehow, without the cooing of the "vendeuses," the creation seemed to give me the distinction and interesting contours of a large bran muffin.

Joan was playing with the caricatured female role of the narcissistic housewife who has nothing but shopping on her mind. She wielded her well-developed ironic sense to demonstrate (to Mrs. Sampson, or anyone not too dim to get it) that she was headed for pursuits beyond the dress shop or beauty parlor.

For all her talent, Joni's disinterest in certain subjects continued to hold her back. "When it comes to mathematics, I got static in the attic," she would later sing on "Ray's Dad's Cadillac." And in fact, she didn't graduate from Aden Bowman on schedule in 1961 because she lacked a few required science and math credits. She's since come to see her inability to make the grade as the struggle of a creative mind in a dull and rote learning environment.

"If something really interests me, I can remember it in great detail. But I went into rebellion in the second grade. I saw [that] the teacher says something, you say it back and you get an A. Give me a question that nobody knows the answer to. So I showed no signs of intelligence in the educational system. I do have a photographic memory for certain things. I can't skim a book and memorize it, but I could read it the night before an exam and get enough to pass. That didn't help me much in school because I could never be forced to remember stuff that doesn't interest me."

Still, this failure haunts her. Any talk of Joni's intellectual influences is sure to bring up a reference to flunking grade twelve. Her every accomplishment seems still to carry the shame of being the dumb kid in the class.

When Tony Simon graduated from the University of Saskatchewan, he took Joan to a graduation party at the home of the dean of the College of Commerce. The dean was just back from Iran and held them in thrall with thrilling stories of his travels. Tony and Joan were supposed to stick around after the party for a big graduation dance, but as usual they cut out of the official function and headed to Waskesiu Lake, where they joined up with a wiener roast and got drunk and sang songs. Joan took a ukulele to the lake in a new role as accompanist. "Out of all the boys nobody played a musical instrument," Tony says. "We were all a bunch of twerps. So she had to provide the background music so there'd be someone to at least accompany our songs." (They often sang songs together at the lake.) No one thought much of Joan's quick facility on an instrument, partly because her dad was musical too, a trumpeter in big bands around town. Besides, as the Waskesiu Lake uke player she performed a service job and her repertoire, which included a bunch of limericks, wasn't exactly high art. (Tony: "She knows more words to dirty songs than any other singer in existence, I can tell you.") No one remembers how well she might have played. Dirty words tend to rob attention from the strumming or picking technique—if there is any—of their accompaniment. She and Tony would later be ostracized from a party in wild-west Calgary for their limericks, stranded without a ride home.

Early on, music was just another part of Joni's tomboy identity, which she carried well into her adolescence and beyond. "I think there are a couple Joans, more than a couple," said Chuck Mitchell, who would meet and marry Joan in 1965. "One is the literal girl, the prairie tomboy. There was a lot of that Joan in the girl—the princess, if you will—I married. Over the years it's got layered over as the historical person, the narrative writer, and the queen evolved."

BEING RAISED IN FARMLAND, one has to become so resourceful at filling in the encompassing emptiness, so steel-willed in one's self-determination, that one's ego can grow pretty big, too. The pragmatic farming community of Saskatoon tended to curb egos by checking colorful or extreme behavior. "I come from a wheat-farming community where it's the tall poppy formula," Joni said. "Stick your head above the crowd, and they'll be happy to lop it off for you!"

The one thing I heard most often when I visited Saskatoon was admiration for the lifelong humility of Bill and Myrtle Anderson, who had a lot to brag about but never did. If prodded, Bill would eventually say his proudest moment was Joan's first big Carnegie Hall appearance. But friends running into Myrtle at the market were always the first to bring up Joan's latest TV appearance, never Myrtle herself. Myrtle's reluctant answer would usually involve something prosaic, like how Joan had eaten only a banana before the concert, the kind of detail that would bring all that fancy show business down to earth. In a place like Saskatoon, where humility is praised, Joan's celebrity called for extra caution from the Andersons because they would have fallen out of favor had they said much about their exceptional daughter. Myrtle quietly put her pride into an extensive scrapbook called "The Life and Times of Roberta Joan Anderson," which was eventually shown at the Mendel Gallery in Saskatoon as part of its "Amazing Childhood of Joni Mitchell" exhibit.

The trouble with this moral code is that modesty about an artistic accomplishment also tends to cut down discussion about art's substance. And in Saskatoon, art is considered a little showy to begin with. So Joan left Saskatchewan as soon as she could for landscapes where a tall poppy might thrive. The story of her early career is well known. She went to art school in Calgary, where she got her first gig singing folk ballads at a club called The Depression. She became pregnant by a fellow art student, Brad McMath, with whom she moved to Toronto. She and McMath split up before the child was born, and Joan made a tormented decision to give up her daughter for adoption. There was a hasty marriage to Chuck Mitchell, and a touring life with him on the folk circuit, for which she assumed the stage name Joni Mitchell. A July 1966 review of one of their shows in the *Saskatoon Star-Phoenix* noted, "much of Joni's material was inspired by her impressions of life on the Prairies." Indeed, Mitchell has often repeated what she told that hometown reviewer about her song "Urge for Going"—that its lyrics "stemmed from the effect the bitter western winter has on prairie residents, and their wish to escape the cold." The

Mitchells both agreed, the reviewer went on, that "Saskatoon and the Prairies contained much that was esthetically beautiful, and Joni said she hopes to continue writing songs based on her Saskatchewan background, and her love of the flat western landscape."

In some respects, of course, it may be unrealistic to try to perceive and analyze landscape in music. Context plays a huge role in how we experience music. When you hear a song or a composition, you are instantly transported back to the time and place in which you first heard and grew to love or hate it. The physical and emotional contexts make almost as deep an impression as the sound of the music itself. Landscape is where everything starts. As author Barry Lopez put it, "Landscape is the culture that contains all human cultures." It may not be possible to pull landscape and music even far enough apart to analyze the impact of one on the other.

Nonetheless, in a special issue of *Canadian Geographic* magazine, songwriters were asked to address the interplay between the country's physical environment and its music. The question was: "How has the Canadian landscape, whether urban or rural, inspired or influenced your music?" Some songwriters were unable or unwilling to answer: Sarah Harmer, from Burlington, Ontario, said she's looking to "express a humble feeling or emotion that vaguely articulates something that is mostly beyond words. That's where music comes in and where it comes from is something you can ask the birds, they may know better." Ontario songwriter Michael Ford helpfully put it this way: "My wife and I take the train all over Canada. Most of the time I've got my face pinned to the glass, drinking in every bluff, slough, river, rock and prairie that passes by with some kind of folk-rock orchestra thrumming through my mind, trying to echo and mirror the swoop and pulse of the land we're crossing."

Ford also mentioned the influence of other landscape-infused songs, that his "sense of the land is informed more by song than by maps or photos. It seems to be the most natural of dialogues." Neil Young recalls being a teenager in Winnipeg and feeding a jukebox all afternoon to hear "Four Strong Winds." "Four Strong Winds" is the quintessential Canadian landscape song and the country's unofficial anthem. Inspired by the migration of farmworkers who followed jobs with the seasons, it tells the story of a relationship straining under the burden of this wandering lifestyle. Its melodic, gentle tune contrasts with the story of the harsh realities that can come with seasonal change. First released by Canadian singers Ian and Sylvia Tyson in 1963, the song has been recorded many times by other artists, including Sarah McLachlan, Bob Dylan, John Denver, the Tragically Hip, Johnny Cash, and, appropriately, Neil Young.

Neil Young understood longing for home. In his song "Helpless," the town in north Ontario "with dream comfort memory to spare" was a familiar place to any Canadian displaced by a move to the city. No matter where he recorded, the center of his albums seemed to be in Manitoba, where he was raised. Few songwriters can match Young's primitive, rambling musical landscapes. On acoustic guitar these landscapes can evoke sanctuary ("Last Trip to Tulsa," "Old Laughing Lady," "Ambulance Blues"); on electric guitar they can sear threateningly ("Down by the River," "Like a Hurricane") or sorrowfully ("On the Beach," "Cowgirl in the Sand"). A friend from Iowa told me he felt like he just *had* to drive out into farmland when he first listened to Young's albums as a teenager. My friend's impulse is a common one, and I think it's a response to Young's gift of translating into music both a landscape's character *and* the feelings it might engender. Listening to Young's songs while driving through the country alone gave my friend the dreamlike experience of merging the music's emotion with a sensation of its loping stride through the surrounding farmland. In a similar way, Young's soundtrack for Jim Jarmusch's *Dead Man* puts you on the open plateaus and within the dense forests that Johnny Depp's character navigates; at the same time the music takes you inside Depp's character, reverberating eerily with his growing understanding that a life in those primitive landscapes is perpetually on the edge of death.

Young lived in Laurel Canyon when he wrote his songs imagining the Canadian homeland, and his nostalgia for home seems to echo across the distance of miles and memory. Of course, back in the days before he'd left Canada, he pined to do just that. Joni Mitchell's "Urge for Going" conveyed that kind of flatland fantasy, a geographical dream of escape from the prairie in the winter months when the "bully winds" move in and the "meadow grass is turning brown." But her original inspiration for the tune had little to do with geography. It came to her after a difficult first performance at the Mariposa Folk Festival in Ontario in August 1965.

> "I wanted to do all my own material, I didn't have much variety. I wasn't very good, and I had a lot of trouble with the audience booing and hissing and saying 'Take your clothes off, sweetheart!' Things like that really shook me up because I didn't know how to counter or how to act. I thought I'd bombed, I wanted to quit, and I was really desperate. On the way back, in the car I wrote a line that said 'It's like running for a train that left the station hours ago / I've got the urge for going, but there's no place left to go.' What I really meant was that the folk movement had died at that point, and that the music I loved had no audience left . . . it was futile and it was silly, and I may as well quit."

Mitchell said she forgot about the line until she cleaned out her guitar case later that fall and came across the scrap of lyric. She often discovered these scraps and couldn't recall the original theme behind them, but the line would stir up a fresh idea, anyway. "I wrote that in August, and the next thing I knew it was September and then October. I was really cold, and I was saying 'I hate winter and I really have the urge for going someplace warm,' and I remembered that line. So I wrote 'Urge for Going' from that." She called it her only protest song, a protest against winter: "And it certainly isn't going to stop winter."

The song transformed a bleak wintry landscape into a site of longing for escape. Her poetic conceit used this scenery to create profundity that anyone, flatlander or no, could understand. Dave Van Ronk heard Mitchell perform "Urge for Going" and began performing it widely. Tom Rush took the song to Judy Collins, who didn't care for it, so he recorded it himself and it became a "turntable hit," or a vinyl single very successful in the radio airplay charts but not so strong in sales. In the folk clubs, Rush popularized Mitchell along with the song. "He'd go into a club and would stand up there and sing my song and build me up and people would get curious, you see," she said. "So he really opened up a whole circuit for me." In 1967, country singer George Hamilton IV cut "Urge for Going" and his version peaked at No. 7 on *Billboard*'s country singles chart. Mitchell didn't put the song on an album of her own until *Hits* in 1996.

"Urge for Going" also resonates with Mitchell's desire to leave her marriage. As she began to enjoy songwriting success, her life with Chuck fell apart. She started looking to other landscapes with great intensity, finding an elemental connection to new places and expressing their sense of meaning for her. It took some time for Mitchell to portray other scenes as compellingly as her homeland. "Night in the city looks pretty to me," she wrote somewhat blandly in 1966 in her ode to Toronto's nighttime cityscape. In 1967, after moving to New York and benefiting from the stimulus of her poet boyfriend Leonard Cohen, she illustrated the city much more convincingly in "Chelsea Morning." In this song, the city bursts through the window of her Chelsea apartment. The sun "poured in like butterscotch" and the "traffic wrote the words" of the song. Here the city is something to go out and "put on," along with the day.

Inspiration came easily to the twenty-five-year-old Mitchell in late-1960s New York. Her quick rise on the music scene got her free passes to clubs, where she saw groups like Cream. She wasn't yet a star—her first album wasn't even out yet—and it was still a thrill when, for example, her friends Larry Hankin and Tony Simon impulsively picked her up at the airport in a limo (that episode would surface in "For Free": "I've got a black limousine and two gentlemen escorting me to the hall"). They went to a screening of the first rushes for D. A. Pennebaker's documentary of the 1967 Monterey Pop Festival, *Monterey Pop*. Stunning performances by artists such as Jimi Hendrix and Janis Joplin introduced many in the screening audience to the West Coast music scene. After the footage of Joplin wrenching her way through "Ball and Chain," nipping from a bottle of bourbon on the side, the room was dead quiet. Finally, somebody said, "Who the fuck was that?!" Laura Nyro's Monterey performance did not make it into the film, but Mitchell was becoming aware of the singer-songwriter then. "I looked to her and took some direction from her. On account of her, I started playing piano again. Some of the things she did were very fresh. Hers was a hybrid of black pop singers—Motown singers—and Broadway musicals, and I like some things also from both those camps." Three decades later Mitchell would refer to Nyro in one of her few flattering comments about a fellow female musician: "Laura Nyro you can lump me in with, because Laura exerted an influence on me."

Also on the bill at Monterey were the Byrds. When David Crosby left the group a few months later, he headed down to Florida where he met Mitchell at the Gaslight South in Miami in October 1967. Their meeting came just in time for Crosby to produce her first recording, *Song to a Seagull*, kind of: Crosby's main contribution was convincing her label, Reprise, to accept her work as she wanted it— simple, with only a guitar and vocal. "I've always been my own producer, from my first album," Mitchell said. "I like the craft of the production end of making a record. I just don't like handing parts of it over to people because they'll make it more popular, more palatable, but they won't make it as daring."

Crosby also convinced her to head out to Los Angeles, and specifically to Laurel Canyon, in 1968. That setting figured into songs like "Ladies of the Canyon," which evokes a quiet late afternoon among Laurel Canyon's winding green hills. She composed parts of *Blue* in her home there, and its piano-accompanied songs are shaded with the intense self-scrutiny of someone who'd finally settled down long enough to take a hard look at herself. In the spring of 1970, she went on the European trip that also so deeply resonates through *Blue*, and incorporated aspects of the Mediterranean into her music, as in her self-described "Matala tuning." At a BBC radio concert in October 1970, Mitchell introduced "Carey" this way: "This instrument is an Appalachian mountain dulcimer. You can tune it any way you want to. I'm going into a tuning now that I call Matala tuning, because I found it as well as the song I'm going to play in Matala, Crete." The melancholy lyrics of the album's title track are deepened by minor keys, and the line "Or let me sail away" is sung over rising intervals in a major key, as if she's floating out to sea on one of the ferries she took in the Mediterranean.

Once Mitchell had been based for a couple of years in Laurel Canyon, her first long-term residence since she'd left Saskatchewan, she began to look back home again. A major feature of the Saskatchewan landscape showed up on her *Blue* recording. In "River" the narrator longs to "quit this crazy scene" of sunny snowless Christmastimes and skate away on the frozen river of her youth. A tone of ironic celebration is set in the first few bars with a minor piano chorus of "Jingle Bells." "I wish I had a river I could skate away on" is a sentiment of romantic escapism: she's sad she "made [her] baby cry" and "say good-bye." "River," like "Both Sides, Now" and "Urge for Going," brings the listener into the singer's psyche, into a soliloquy delivered as a stream of recollection and regret. The song also says something different about what certain landscapes offer the self. If "Urge for Going" is a dream of literal, geographical escape, "River" is a return to interiority afforded by a particular place, an involution or spiral into subjectivity, the narrator skating herself back to a familiar childlike comfort in melancholy on a frozen river.

The Canadian landscape experience has often been treated in the country's literature as beleaguered humankind's attempt to preserve its integrity in the face of an alien, encompassing nature. By contrast, the narrator of "River" struggles to preserve her integrity in the face of a strange and confining culture, urban California during the holidays. For a flatlander, unrestricted panoramas, vistas, or the frozen path of a long, wide river, offer powerful prospects—a place where you could find safety in seeing without being seen, in unburdening yourself without burdening anyone else. If Mitchell's narrator had a river to skate away on, she'd have the possibility of refuge, not just from failed romance but also from her "selfish" and "sad" self. Mitchell's piano accompaniment has the slow, graceful rhythm of ice-skating, and its minor harmony achieves the somber dignity for which the lyrics strive. There are filmic images: with "teach my feet to fly," a sustained vocal run on the word "fly" takes to the air like a skater in a flying spin. It's as vivid as Ralph Vaughan Williams's sound of a bird soaring through the English countryside in "The Lark Ascending." Wistfulness for the sanctity of solitude during the holidays made "River" a new holiday classic, especially after the release of popular cover versions by Sarah McLachlan and James Taylor. "Look how many people identify with that song at Christmastime—everybody!" Joni told me. "How many people go through Christmas happy? More are miserable than not. And that song, every year more people sing it with great authenticity. I've never heard anybody sing that song that it didn't sound like it was about themselves."

"River" offers a musical illustration of movement through landscape, a mood of a place. At the end of her Blue Period, on *Hejira*, Mitchell went deeper into her native landscape, merging the feeling and vision of open spaces into her music; the lyrics of "Song for Sharon" maintain the subject/narrator still has her "eyes on the land and the sky." Finally, at her most grandiosely picturesque in the orchestral masterpiece on *Don Juan's Reckless Daughter*, "Paprika Plains," Mitchell depicted "sky-oriented people" like her, who are "geared to changing weather." Its sparse, shifting Copland- and Debussy-esque piano harmonies alternate with orchestral stretches involving descending string passages that evoke rain, flutes as flocks of birds, and dissonant intervals as charged as the air of a thunderstorm. Back in her hometown, the lyrics attest, they "would have cleared the floor just to watch the rain come down." The episodic composition dramatizes both the fierce flare-up of a plains squall and the mesmerizing effect it had on the locals.

Over the years Mitchell has found refuge in her second home on British Columbia's Sunshine Coast. ("I found the flattest piece of property to buy on the Sunshine Coast," she remarked, when I asked if she's still connected to her flatlander origins.) "One Week Last Summer," an instrumental on her 2007 album *Shine*, shows Mitchell has never stopped translating landscape and its inhabitation of her into music. Here are her liner notes to the piece:

"I stepped outside of my little house and stood barefoot on a rock. The Pacific Ocean rolled towards me. Across the bay, a family of seals sprawled on the kelp uncovered by the low tide. A blue heron honked overhead. All around the house the wild roses were blooming. The air smelled sweet and salty and loud with crows and bees. My house was clean. I had food in the fridge for a week. I sat outside 'til the sun went down.

"That night the piano beckoned for the first time in ten years. My fingers found these patterns which express what words could not. This song poured out while a brown bear rummaged through my garbage cans.

"The song has seven verses constructed for the days of that happy week. On Thursday the bear arrives."

3

Art Songs

"SUMMERTIME IN ENGLAND" IS VAN MOR-
rison's hallucinatory tribute to his literary ances-
tors. It began as a poem about Wordsworth and
Coleridge's historic trip to England's Lake District.
It became a fifteen-minute epic song with an improvised literary roll call. Wordsworth and Coleridge
were smoking up in Kendal by the lakeside, he sings.
Yeats corresponded with Lady Gregory. T. S. Eliot
chose England and the ministry, he tells us, and have
you heard about William Blake? A midsong shift to
an organ church fugue with swelling strings empha-

sizes the holiness of this lineage and underscores Van Morrison's own shifts in narrative consciousness. He intersperses writerly episodes in England with a day of his own in the country, where all that history creates a silence he can feel. Where he wants to show his lover "it ain't why, why, why. It just is."

A generation before, Van Morrison would have most likely paid tribute to England's literary history in verse. He might have let his hair grow long and tangled, inhabited down-and-out quarters, and produced short literary works of great intensity. Instead, along with a number of other poetic sorts in the '60s, he did all that and also set those literary works to music. The postwar rise of popular music, especially the folk movements in New York's Greenwich Village and Toronto's Yorkville, lured many would-be poets into songwriting. As these artists emerged in the 1960s so did various terms for them. "Song-poet" was popular for a while, but it was "singer-songwriter" that stuck. It got across the idea of writing to sing and singing to write. The singer-songwriter phenomenon in effect returned poetry it to its roots: back in the Middle Ages, troubadours sang their verses as tuneful metaphysical conceits. And the very notion of the lyrical in poetry goes back even farther, to antiquity, when words were sung to the lyre's accompaniment.

Of course, any discussion of song lyrics as literature usually brings up a big question: Can songwriters make it as poets or storytellers? Can lyrics stand on the page, apart from music? Evaluative criteria for this debate have always been a little slippery. What is and is not poetry, after all? And the matter has become less urgent over the years as pop culture has made its mark in even the most pristine reaches of the academy. Joni Mitchell is now the recipient of honorary doctorates. Song lyrics are so canonized that it seems they're almost as likely to show up in American Literature courses as Whitman's *Leaves of Grass*.

But the literary world's smoldering resentment of songwriters' pretensions to poetry is always ready to flare up again. A combination of outrage and disbelief greeted the 2007 publication of Mitchell's lyrics to "Bad Dreams" as a poem in *The New Yorker*.

> *In the dark*
> *A shining ray*
> *I heard a three-year-old boy say*
> *Bad Dreams are good*
> *In the Great Plan*

The theme is worthy of Yeats, but as many noted, the execution, with its easy rhyme and banal formula, suggests the indulgent syntax of a proud grandmother—which is exactly what it is. The song was based on something Mitchell heard her "old soul" grandson say. Even many of Mitchell's most devoted fans regretted the publication of this "poem" for other reasons, since it was included thanks to her legendary status in late middle age rather than on its literary merit. It was far from her most interesting or poetic work.

Literary influence abounds in songwriting: the scholar Richard Sutherland has spoken of Jim Morrison and Patti Smith drawing inspiration from poet Arthur Rimbaud; Bruce Springsteen's obvious debt to John Steinbeck and Thomas Wolfe; the Rolling Stones' copping the idea for "Sympathy for the Devil" from nineteenth-century French poet Charles Baudelaire. No matter what their influences, lyrics have no duty to work as poetry, unless of course they're presented as such, and increasingly, they are. The idea of "lyrics as poetry" was popular in the 1960s, then reemerged in the past decade, when books of lyrics by Patti Smith, Paul McCartney, Mitchell, Jewel, and other songwriters have been published for a general audience. The very existence of these books is a kind of claim to literary legitimacy. Critics who deny that legitimacy generally make this distinction: poems twist and turn public language to reveal interior truths, while songs unite audiences in collective truths. Poems undo rhetoric to reveal deeper meanings; songs use rhetoric to uphold accepted meanings.

But this distinction doesn't quite hold up for autobiographical songwriting, which both loosens common language to expose personal intimacies in lyrics and unites listeners in the collective truth and kinetic force of music. Still, since music is very much a part of a songwriter's message, one larger critical argument does remain valid: if you read many songwriters' lyrics apart from their intended musical settings, even landmark compositions can seem simply thin, lacking in wit, depth, or energy. Whether it's because we associate song lyrics with musical accompaniment, or because they need it, lyrics come to life with music.

Take, for example, how music and lyrics combine for a visceral listening experience in Mitchell's "A Case of You." The song opens with a conversation between lovers. The narrator's lover claims to be constant; the narrator responds that he's only constantly in the darkness and admits that for her part, he can find her in the bar. It's a funny and self-effacing line. But for all the verse's clever wordplay and sardonic smirk, it isn't the stuff of great poetry. In the second verse of "A Case of You," Joni sings:

> I am a lonely painter
> I live in a box of paints
> I'm frightened by the devil
> And I'm drawn to those ones that ain't afraid.

The departure from the rhyme scheme with "afraid" illustrates the boldness she describes. That *is* poetic expression. Still, the lyrics only come to resonate with real power when you hear the ensuing chorus. There, in the line, "I could drink a case of you and I would still be on my feet," Mitchell matches emphatically strummed single chords to each word of the phrase, "on my feet." Music animates the line so evocatively that any child could tell you the song is about standing strong, no matter how drunk with feeling one might be. This combined force of words and music gives the song its appeal and meaning. Having used words and music so inextricably, Mitchell was particularly struck by a comment from writer Meghan Daum, who is a huge fan: "She told me, as a writer, she'd be writing something in her book, and her great frustration was that there wasn't a chord sweeping up to punctuate the apex of her idea!"

I'll leave arguments about the absolute poetic value of song lyrics to the literary critics. In Mitchell's case, as with the best songwriters, it's both poetic expression and musical expressionism that make her work so powerful. "Poetry is news that stays news," Ezra Pound once remarked. Mitchell's songs have had currency for decades, and that's partly due to a true union of musical form and lyrical content in her work. "My words and music are locked together," Mitchell acknowledged. She interlinked music and words in an effort to bring a new level of artistry to the American pop song, she said, and draws an analogy to the innovation of Canadian figure skater Toller Cranston.

"When I watched him I used to get a lump in my throat. He won the bronze [at the 1976 Winter Olympics] and about four years later he'd already opened up figure skating and took it from being a curio, like a sport almost, to an art form. He said, 'All I did was bring dance, like jazz dance to the ice.' And that's basically all he did. Maybe I did the same thing with the song. What I did was bring just a little more detail to pop lyrics like

'I feel blue,' for example, pairing it with more specific character and metaphors and making the music actually feel blue with what I call my chords of inquiry. I was trying to grow up the American pop song into an art song. And then bring a level of theater or jazz to my performance."

JONI MITCHELL WROTE "A Case of You" in part for her one-time lover Leonard Cohen, a rare songwriter who could and did make it as a poet. Cohen is also the only songwriter other than Dylan whom Mitchell admits as an influence: "Those two are my pacesetters," she says, definitively. An accomplished literary figure in Canada, Cohen had already published acclaimed collections of poetry, including *Let Us Compare Mythologies* and *Flowers for Hitler*, as well as novels such as *Beautiful Losers*, before he recorded his debut album in 1967. Just why a man with such an unexceptional singing voice and fine literary talents would be compelled to lend them to music has spawned a number of apocryphal origin stories. A Canadian favorite goes like this: In the early '60s, when Cohen was just a poet and hadn't yet begun to sing, he went to a Bob Dylan concert in Montreal. "This guy is so fucking bad!" he exclaimed on the way out. "If that son of a bitch can make a living singing, then so can I!" Bob Dylan had shown Mitchell that songs could be written about anything; maybe he helped Cohen see that even a guy without much of a singing voice could find a greater range of expression in song. Canadians also relish the notion that Ian Tyson was inspired to write the country's folk anthem "Four Strong Winds" after he heard Dylan's "Blowin' in the Wind," because Tyson decided he could do better.

Cohen and Mitchell met backstage in the summer of 1967 at the Newport Folk Festival, in Judy Collins's songwriter's workshop. Cohen had not yet released an album but had already gained some songwriting renown through Collins's performance of his song "Suzanne." The song was a character portrait of a woman that raised sensuality to a spiritual pursuit and the first of Cohen's many songs that would shape a listening generation's understanding of desire. Cohen brought his decidedly romantic and personal poetic voice to his music, and it made a huge impression on Mitchell.

"When I broke my marriage from Chuck Mitchell, Chuck Mitchell had had a degree in literature and I had flunked grade twelve. So he had the pride of the educated and he basically thought I was stupid. I came out of the marriage with a chip on my shoulder. Shortly after that, I met Leonard and I said to him, 'I'm illiterate, basically. I haven't read anything, give me a reading list.'"

As Mitchell remembers, Leonard told her she was writing songs very well for someone who hadn't read anything, and reading might actually detract from the originality of her songwriting. She pressed, and he gave her a reading list that included Lorca, Camus, and the *I Ching*, a book she describes as a "lifelong companion." Cohen's worldliness intrigued Mitchell, she often says, and the depth of revelation in his songs showed her how opulently she could mine her own experience in music. She commemorated their meeting in "That Song About the Midway," when Cohen "stood out like a ruby in a black man's ear."

Cohen and Mitchell were soon spending a lot of time together, and by the time they cohosted a songwriter's workshop at the Mariposa Folk Festival outside Toronto, a month after meeting, they were officially an item. The two expatriate Canadians had both recently moved to New York and shared a penchant for restlessness, both geographically and in matters of the heart. Aesthetically both were too earnest to join the counterculture in celebrating the social underbelly for its own sake, and they were too conservative to revere dysfunction as an artistic end, as Allen Ginsberg did in *Howl*, for example. "I never really liked that avant-garde period, in music or painting, that pocket of creativity in the late '50s," Mitchell told me. "I didn't really like it in painting or literature, so maybe I'm not a good judge of it. That period where it gets too abstract and too neurotic, you know? I still think that an artist's duty is to inspire, not to give in to neuroses."

Mitchell was primed to appreciate Cohen's careful lyrical craftsmanship and absorbed it very quickly. When in 1968 Mitchell released her debut album, *Song to a Seagull*, Cohen's sensibility seemed to be so deeply a part of it that the *Rolling Stone* reviewer couldn't even make sense of the connection; he simply heard Mitchell's work embodying Cohen's most well-known song character: "Joni Mitchell is Leonard Cohen's 'Suzanne': she shows you where to look among the garbage and the flowers." She was his word made flesh, somehow. In retrospect, Cohen's influence on Mitchell is much clearer than that. She herself acknowledged that he gave her a model for approaching lyrics:

> "I think I'm rather Cohen influenced. I wrote a song called 'Marcie,' which I don't think would have happened if it hadn't been for 'Suzanne,' which is another character sketch song. The total character sketch of a person, many people have done it. Dylan wrote 'Hattie Carroll' . . . but I'm not a political person. . . . 'Suzanne,' of course, is going to be more the kind of song that is going to influence me, because it's more romantic, a romantic character sketch rather than something done for dramatic purposes."

Cohen liked to dismiss "Suzanne" as "reportage," but he didn't mean it was faithful to facts so much as in narrative form; the song's profile of an acquaintance was seriously transformed for art. Rich details and ambiguity give Suzanne the character and "Suzanne" the song compelling complexity. She wears rags and feathers from Salvation Army counters. "You know that she's half crazy / But that's why you want to be there."

Mitchell's attempt at a similar portrait in "Marcie," which she wrote in 1968, is the simple tragedy of an everywoman. Marcie, who wears a "coat of flowers," has sorrow that "needs a man," and her melancholy grows throughout the song, as "red" and "green" go from symbolizing a candy store's "sweet" and "sour" to symbolizing the "angry" and "jealous" moods of lost love, and with it, fallen innocence. Suzanne is a woman whose seductive character brings one further into the world through love; Marcie's experience of love takes her out of the world. Both songs are, however, unabashedly sentimental, a fact of which Mitchell was well aware at the time of their release. "We Canadians are a bit more nosegay, more Old-Fashioned Bouquet than Americans," she told *The New York Times* in 1969. "We're poets because we're such reminiscent kind of people. I love Leonard's sentiments, so I've been strongly influenced by him."

Alongside "Marcie" and rather fey selections such as "Sisotowbell Lane," which has the atmosphere of Louisa May Alcott's *Little Women* crashing a Dungeons & Dragons game, there were some more fully realized pieces on Mitchell's debut album. Its opening song, "I Had a King," evokes both the waning folk scene and Mitchell's failed first marriage: her recording career actually begins with a commitment to charting her disillusionment. The song's medieval setting of castles and carriages is a façade for its real location, revealed late in the song—a tenement apartment in some modern city where bad love has stripped the room of any comfort. The musicologist Lloyd Whitesell has analyzed the highly wrought poetic construction of various of Mitchell's songs. His diagram of "I Had a King" shows how her work recalls Cohen's as she arranges rhymes within lines to form a densely interlocking structure.

I had a king in a tenement castle	a			
Lately he's taken to painting				
the pastel walls brown	a	b		
He's taken the curtains down		b		
He's swept with the broom of contempt	c	d		
And the rooms have an empty ring	c	d	e	
He's cleaned with the tears of an actor	f	g		
Who fears for the laughter's sting	f	g	e	

The end-rhymes of lines 1, 4 and 6 are paired with words internal to the subsequent lines. As Whitesell notes, the ornate verbal pattern reflects the deliberately precious metaphorical conceit, heightening the message of disillusionment underneath. The song's minimal accompaniment, intimate singing, and complex, layered lyrical meanings are Cohen-esque. In her performance of "I Had a King," Mitchell's voice sometimes projects his bardic gravity, but more often she achieves a graceful simplicity that it would take two decades and a Zen Buddhist practice for Cohen to achieve. As a teenager, Mitchell had loved the gorgeous tunes of '40s crooners, despite the sometimes shallow nature of their lyrics. Her songs carry something of those tunes as she sings long, free-ranging lines that swoop down and soar up, unlike the flatter melodies used by Cohen or Bob Dylan as mere background to their lyrics.

Cohen and Mitchell's affair ended after a few months, though it continued to have a big influence on the subject matter and aesthetics of her lyrics. "The Gallery," on her next album, *Clouds*, portrayed Cohen as a manipulative collector of women.

> *I have no heart, that's what you said*
> *You said, I can be cruel*
> *But let me be gentle with you*

Here Mitchell exposes Cohen's apparent self-disclosure as a way of realizing his desires. *Ladies of the Canyon* came out in 1970, a couple of years after their breakup, and by then Mitchell was of a more peaceful mind as she again revisited Leonard as a character. In "Rainy Night House," she gently parodied him with some of his own religious imagery, as a "holy man on the FM radio." Mitchell sings solo to a simple piano accompaniment, but overdubs her vocals to create the striking sound of the entire "upstairs choir" in which she says she "sing[s] soprano" in the song. *Ladies of the Canyon* also features Cohen in "The Priest," where she mocks his tendency to remain barren of lasting commitment while loving so many.

It was four years after their affair that Mitchell most honestly paid tribute to Cohen, on *Blue*, her most truehearted recording. On "A Case of You," she scoffs at his idea of himself as "constant as a northern star," but implies that love is not lost when it can be re-created in memory and in poetry.

> *You said, "love is touching souls"*
> *Surely you touched mine*
> *'Cause part of you pours out of me*
> *In these lines from time to time.*

She then demonstrates this ongoing effect of Cohen's art and love: "You're in my blood like holy wine," she sings, transubstantiating the holy into sexual love as Cohen so often did in his lyrics.

In interviews, Cohen has affirmed the fineness of Mitchell's work, listing her among his group of chosen songwriters who emerged in the 1960s: "Like the Talmud says, there's good wine in every generation," Cohen quoted, in yet another characteristic pairing of the aesthetic and religious. Mitchell's impact on him grew as his songwriting began to make the music part of its message as opposed to relying primarily on the lyrics—as in the song "Hallelujah," his hymn to lost love, which was first recorded in 1984. He sings of a "secret chord" that "goes like this": "The fourth, the fifth / The minor fall, the major lift." In the musical accompaniment to "the fourth, the fifth, the minor fall, the major lift," the chords move as described in the lyrics. It's a Mitchell-inspired moment of musical onomatopoeia; she'd been matching music to lyrical meanings since her first record, when she used minor and major shifts to shade the lyrics of "Tin Angel."

Mitchell has been more ambivalent about Cohen's influence. In 1976, she forthrightly told an interviewer that Cohen "held a mirror up" to her work and "with no verbal instructions" showed her how to "plumb the depth of her experiences." But later she reduced him to a "boudoir poet," and now dismisses him as a derivative one at that.

> "I used to give Leonard and Dylan credit for growing up the pop song. After I read Camus and Lorca, I started to realize that Leonard had stolen a lot of their lines—I mean, he handed me the source of his plagiarism in the reading list he gave me. That was very disappointing to me. 'Walk me to the corner, our steps . . .' That's a direct lift out of Camus."

At age sixty-five, Mitchell has become a social commentator in song and has long been a lyricist of much more than personal anecdote. She tends to see things differently in retrospect as her understanding is tainted by bitterness over the music industry's failure to support the innovation of her work—work like "The Jungle Line," which incorporated Moog synthesizers and a sample of Burundi drummers, a pretty exotic combination in 1975 when it was recorded. The song's beautifully sinister lyrics were somewhat buried in the ambitious musical mix.

It took Cohen himself to recover the poetry from the hectic sound of "The Jungle Line," as he did in a clear, laconic intonation for Herbie Hancock's reinterpretation on the Grammy Award–winning *The Joni Letters*. In his way, Cohen has remained faithful to Mitchell over the years, and certainly more loyal in his regard. After praising Mitchell's work, he allowed this: "But we have a special kind of feeling for the singers that we used to make love to."

I pressed Joni to admit she also still appreciates Cohen's work, that he's his own poet on songs like "Hallelujah."

"Of course I'll always love some of Leonard's writing," she conceded. "There's a lot of Leonard in those songs." She couldn't resist some pointed humor, though. "He owns the word 'naked body,' that's his. I don't think he can write a song without using 'naked body.'"

JONI MITCHELL DIDN'T have formal musical training and never learned to read music. Her musical vocabulary is purely expressionistic, with emotions or ideas taking the form of "weird chords" or "chords of inquiry," as she calls them. These weird or unorthodox chords are a necessary foil for her lyrics: "Americans seem to like their tragedy minor and their happiness major, and the most they can handle is a seventh and anything after that is weird," Mitchell told Chris Douridas on KCRW in Santa Monica. "Whereas, like, I invent these open tunings that I play and these modalities, a lot of times specifically for the lyric, trying to avoid tragic statements underscored with minors, you know. That's generally the pattern." Open or alternate tunings are the method through which Mitchell affects such a prismatic rendering of musical emotions; these tunings are what make her music resonate with feeling.

In the mid-'60s, folk singer-songwriter Eric Andersen showed Mitchell something called "open-G" tuning on the guitar. Over the next few years, Mitchell used the technique to quietly revolutionize the instrument. Guitar music, of course, depends on tuning, or how tightly the strings are pulled in relation to one another. Beginning guitar students learn to use standard tuning, or E–A–D–G–B–E, from the lowest-pitched string to the highest. Standard tuning offered a compromise between simple, easy fingering for chords and the facility to play common scales from a single hand position.

This system is at first adequate for most musicians, because there are many combinations of finger positions or notes that can be used to create any chord. Some musicians find lasting contentment in standard tuning. The trouble is, for other artists, standard tunings can invite inertia, a hollow reverberation of old musical discoveries. "You know, in standard tuning it seemed to me that it had been mined out, so no matter what colors you put together, you'd heard it," Mitchell has said. "It was like it had all been laid out. So by twiddling the strings and going off into this adventure into the unknown, you coughed up fresh chordal progressions and so on to get away from that." Alternate tunings require new fingerings, and that physical variation can open up a composer's approach and inspire different musical ideas.

As with most innovation, the technique of open tuning isn't especially difficult, it's just radically different from the standard technique. And alternate tuning alone doesn't necessarily guarantee innovation. Many blues musicians use it for the ease of sliding back and forth on the fret board from basic triad chord to basic triad chord without changing fingerings. But Mitchell was looking to paint emotions through sound, so she had special uses for the technique. "Immediately, it gave me a sense I could get at the melodies I heard in my head," she has said. "I only wrote two songs in standard tuning in my whole life. If I didn't learn that tuning I probably would have quit or I would have gone to the piano." Her open tunings on the guitar were the equivalent of getting inside a piano and restringing it. It was as if she created a whole new instrument, and through that, entirely new ways of feeling in music.

Open tunings gave Mitchell, not an exceptionally deft guitarist, the freedom of innovation, and allowed her to work around the nerve damage in her hands from her childhood polio attack. Mitchell wrote "Little Green" in 1967, and the open-G tuning is youthfully experimental, giving the song shades of spring. By the time she wrote "This Flight Tonight," which appeared on *Ladies of the Canyon* in 1971, she'd progressed to tunings like G–G–D–G–B–D, with the two lowest-pitched strings a leaping octave apart, providing a soaring range that painted a picturesque backdrop for a song about flight. She's worked with more than fifty tunings throughout her career, a broad and varied palette. Jazz composer and saxophonist Wayne Shorter, who's played on Mitchell's albums since the 1970s, recently said, "Joni didn't play the guitar with an academic or clinical approach. It was like she was going where her vocabulary guitar-wise took her. And there was variation. They put the music in front of me [in the studio], and then I'd start playing and close my eyes instead of looking at a B or D7 chord, because it wasn't actually those chords anyway. It was an inversion of something, and the chord would sound like it was from Asia. Some other chords sounded minor-ish, or besides minor, you could say melancholy, sentimental, questioning. Some harmonic chords you'd hear in Stravinsky, Bartók, those kinds of chords." Musicians tend to have a special appreciation of Mitchell's pure expressionism: most artists would kill to make music in which every note and word is spirited and shaped by feeling.

The wildness in her guitar tunings and their reworking of harmonic laws is all the more intriguing for its untutored, instinctive basis. She never studied music theory, and carefully maintained her musical illiteracy while listening to and absorbing work of great sophistication. And though there was a practical impetus for her open tunings—they were a way to reduce stress on her left hand—they manifested quite unexpectedly into a bounty of unheard musical intervals. For years, Joni's "chords of inquiry" would confound many of the rock- and folk-based musicians in her bands. It wasn't until musicians such as Jaco Pastorius and Wayne Shorter later interpreted, analyzed, and named these "chords" that her true innovation was appreciated.

In her music up to and including *Ladies of the Canyon*, there was, however, still something missing. "The music that I was making was very different from the music I loved," Mitchell told me. "I actually had a black sense of feel." On *Blue*, Mitchell began to integrate the music she loved into the music she made. The jazz she'd admired since her teenage days, for example, influenced the title track. "I think the first few notes on 'Blue' [the title track] sound like a muted trumpet tone," she said. "Just the opening part, it's very influenced by Miles. It's not exactly mimicking him, but absolutely the tone of that opening phrase comes from listening to Miles." While her vocal tone and phrasing reflect Miles Davis, her piano chords recall classical impressionists like Chopin, Debussy and again, Rachmaninoff. Piano chords in certain songs from *Blue*, such as "My Old Man," sometimes serve no harmonic purpose in the traditional sense; these chords set the color and mood of the piece, and traditional ideas of release and tension are suspended for a dreamy flow of ideas. Those ideas reflect the two earliest pieces of music she loved: Rachmaninoff's popular 18th Variation from "Rhapsody on a Theme by Paganini" and Edith Piaf's "Les Trois Cloches."

On "My Old Man," her lover is the "warmest chord I ever heard." But then he's gone and "the bed's too big" and "the frying pan's too wide." Over and over again on the album she "tosses off the beautiful, offbeat Raymond Carver–style snapshots of love on the rocks," as one reviewer said. Joni's ability to capture complex emotional scenes in only a few lines of song would later give her trouble when she composed for film. "They always ask me to write something for a soundtrack and then reject me, and you know why?" she asked me. "Because I tell the whole story, the whole movie." On the self-contained songs of *Blue*, her painterly images made each track into a short story or film in its own right.

As the album arabesques through romantic hope and disillusionment, it maintains dramatic unity and sustains musical mood. All elements of the compositions are sensitive to the emotional detail of the lyrics, more than ever before in her work. In form *Blue* is a classical song cycle, with interconnected lyrics set to related songs that enhance each other in a truly unique way. In early March of 1971, the masters for *Blue* were sent by Reprise to their record plants. But word came down that Mitchell had decided to recall the master tape and substitute two new songs—"All I Want" and "The Last Time I Saw Richard"—for "Urge for Going," which appeared in 1972 as the B-side to "You Turn Me On, I'm a Radio" and "Hunter," which never appeared on record. The addition of "The Last Time I Saw Richard" changes the record substantially.

It's been assumed by many critics and fans that "Richard" is Mitchell's first husband, Chuck Mitchell. Biographer Karen O'Brien even refers to the protagonist of the song as "Richard/Chuck." Certain lyrical details do fit Joni's first husband. Chuck stayed on in Detroit for a few years after Joni left. He was raised near the city, in Rochester, and his parents lived there. From there on, the details can't be so easily attributed to Chuck. The woman he married next was a waitress at Coconut Grove's club The Flick, and went on to become a registered nurse—never the song's "figure skater." Chuck claimed to have had no familiarity with the song, and after listening, was sure it was not about him: "I have no idea who Richard is, but betcha a nickel he's not me."

Chuck was right, as Joni finally confirmed. She'd never said anything about the song referring specifically to Chuck, but then she never attaches a song to any one person, as she believes that doing so would diminish its resonance for listeners. "It doesn't matter who the guy is," she said. "Too much attention is put on the gossip and not on the art. It doesn't matter who it is—it's a friend of mine, not a romantic interest." As the conversation continued, Mitchell felt the need to get explicit. "Okay, this is where that song came from," she said. "Patrick Sky, a fellow folksinger, said to me one night in a bar in New York, 'Oh, Joni, you're a hopeless romantic. There's only one way for you to go. Hopeless cynicism.' And that was it. That one little nugget became that song." In the song, Richard marries a figure skater and becomes a homebody. "Patrick Sky married a figure skater and didn't go to the bar anymore. So you assume he went for domesticity. And there's a little dark humor thrown in there—he bought her a dishwasher and he drinks at home with the lights up high instead of at last call."

On *Blue*, Mitchell's flatlander ability to face extremes became a willingness to explore and honestly reveal her feelings and experiences. Still, she was very careful about her delivery. Her dense phrasing pushes at the structure of "Richard," spilling words out over lines, giving the subtle impression that this joy and sorrow might be too much for her skin and bones to contain. But there was little glamour or melodrama in her delivery. "Melodrama I avoid like the plague, even on sad songs," Joni said. "I may indulge it on one note. You don't want to be maudlin. You want to attain an impact in your read, a theatricality in the right places, but don't sad down the whole thing into one big monochromatic sad." In "Richard," Mitchell begins to experiment with jazz vocal technique, in particular with blue notes—notes that are sung or played at a lower pitch than notated, maybe just a semitone or less, but enough to push the notes' expressions into other meanings. Early on, jazz and blues musicians made blue notes out of the third and seventh notes of a scale, though any note can be made blue. In the '40s, bebop musicians started bluing the fifth note of a scale, or fooling around with flattened fifths, and on Blue, Mitchell does the same. For example, when she sings "love so sweet," her flattening of the phrase's notes complicates the lyric, making the meaning bittersweet. The song's blue notes give its sound a bluish cast that approaches synesthesia—in my listening experience, anyway.

With its exquisite transparency of self, *Blue* was a turning point for Joni Mitchell. Though her later albums may be more compelling musically, and other work may have as much depth and introspection, *Blue* has more raw emotion and nerve than all the rest. Most reviewers recognized this immediately. "Joni Mitchell's greatest gift is that of being uncommonly receptive to the world around her," wrote one reviewer. "She has a unique way of creating from her experiences meaningful songs with intense images and feelings." Most critics had no trouble recognizing that Mitchell had put herself on the line: "In portraying herself so starkly, she has risked the ridiculous to achieve the sublime."

Blue helped make Joni an artist's artist. Madonna has said: "I would have to say of all the women I've heard, she had the most profound effect on me from a lyrical point of view." Led Zeppelin's "Going to California" was written about the band members' infatuation with Joni. In live performances, Plant would sometimes sing, "To find a queen without a king, they say she plays guitar and cries and sings," then he'd say "Joni." Annie Lennox wrote in her liner notes to Nonesuch's Joni Mitchell tribute album, "The expression of her extraordinary artistic powers gave me the blueprint and inspiration to pursue my own creative calling. (A fairly audacious enterprise indeed.) Joni's voice and songs have haunted me ever since the moment I first heard them in the early '70s. The poetic genius of her lyrical imagery tangled with my brain, and I was challenged to try to follow suit. Truth be known . . . there is NO ONE who can come even near."

One reviewer worried about Joni's art growing more in-

above Fort MacLeod, Alberta, December 1943: A month-old Joni with her father, Bill Anderson. Bill was a Link Trainer Instructor for No. 2 Flying Instructor School at Royal Canadian Air Force Station Pearce. *Photo courtesy of Maidstone Museum.*

right Fort MacLeod, Alberta, November 1944: On the back of this photo Joni's mother, Myrtle, wrote: "It was the first time she had seen snow. She had fun making footprints in it." *Photo courtesy of Maidstone Museum.*

left Maidstone, 1946: Joni stimulating her illusions on a backyard swing built by her father. *Photo courtesy of Maidstone Museum.*

right Maidstone, 1946: Sharon Bell, Joni, Myrtle.
Photo courtesy of Maidstone Museum.

Maidstone, November 7, 1946: Joni "weaving a course of grace and havoc" with fellow partygoers at her third birthday. Back row (left to right): Sherilyn Carson, Sharon Bell, Marilyn McGee, Vernon Burkett; front row (left to right): Leonard Burkett, Joni, Billie Warwick. *Photo courtesy of Maidstone Museum.*

above Maidstone: Another gathering with friends. Back row (left to right): Vernon Burkett, Joni, Sherilyn Carson, Sharon Bell, Billie Warwick; front row: (standing) Leonard Burkett, (sitting) Randy Burlingham. *Photo courtesy of Maidstone Museum.*

right Maidstone, 1947: Marilyn McGee and Joni playing dress up. *Photo courtesy of Maidstone Museum.*

Outtakes from a November 1968 photo shoot for *Vogue* magazine.
Photos courtesy of the Jack Robinson Archive.

Spring 1970: Joni and fellow cave denizen David Hodes with the "bright red devil," Cary Raditz, in front of the Mermaid Café in Matala. *Collection of David Hodes, photographer unknown.*

left Spring 1970: The Matala caves, Crete. *Collection of David Hodes, photographer unknown.*

right Spring 1970: Joni at the Mermaid Café. *Collection of David Hodes, photographer unknown.*

Joni Mitchell's new album will mean more to some than to others.

Amy Foster, twenty-three years old and quietly beautiful, was sitting in her orange inflatable chair listening to Neil Young's second album and toying indifferently with the enormous antique ring on the index finger of her left hand. Mostly she was trying with the usual lack of success to avoid lapsing into that state of bored listlessness she'd found herself in so frequently of late as she waited for the Country Store delivery boy to arrive with her groceries and RIT, with which she planned to pass the evening by tie-dyeing some curtains for her '64 Chevy camper.

To say simply that she had been under the weather these past few days would have been to wildly understate the case. Indeed, ever since she had been told on Sunday night by a mutual acquaintance that David, who had left her a month ago in favor of some chick he had met at the Jeans West shop he managed, had up and married, Amy had been more than a little inclined to chucking everything in the back of her camper and taking off for indefinite points north to try to get her head

back together. Today, of course, was no exception: "I'm incredibly down, man," she observed to herself as the turntable's arm lifted quietly off "Down By The River" and someone began knocking impatiently at the back door.

It was the delivery boy. After depositing her groceries on the kitchen table he stopped to admire the Van Morrison collage she had made, so Amy offered him some tea. This he accepted with a gracious and endearing toothy smile.

As they sat in the living room sipping Constant Comment with orange honey mixed in and listening to side one of Deja Vu he, whose name turned out to be Barry, took out a concise little joint, lit it and took a couple of polite hits, and passed it over to Amy. "Mellow," she responded, her spirits lifting slightly.

"Hey, you really have a far-out system here," Barry commented in reference to her stereo set-up as she handed the joint back. "Do you think we could listen to some of Joni Mitchell's new album on it," for he had purchased Ladies

of the Canyon at the Music Hall just that afternoon. "Hey, groovy," agreed Amy, who had not even realized that the album had been released.

So Barry brought it in and placed it on the turntable. By the time "For Free" was over they were both quite mellow indeed. As much as they downed her by reminding her all too vividly of her now-irrevocably-consummated relationship with David, "Willy" and "Conversation" were somehow reassuring—there was someone else, even another canyon lady, who really knew. Amy began to feel a little better.

By the time "Circle Game" had finished, Amy was no longer dejectedly contemplating splitting for Oregon. In fact, she could scarcely wait for the sun to get through setting so she could drive up to the top of Lookout and watch Los Angeles twinkle beneath the indigo April sky.

Joni Mitchell's *Ladies of the Canyon*
On Reprise albums and tapes

While Joni was in Europe, Reprise Records was promoting *Ladies of the Canyon* with this advertorial short story: a lovelorn hippie girl finds solace in the combination of a strong joint and Joni's new record.

August 29, 1970: Joni performing at the Isle of Wight Festival,
East Afton Farm, Godshille, England. The calm before the storm.
Photo by Bernard Rouan.

August 29, 1970: Joni commanding the beast to lie down at the
Isle of Wight Festival. *Photo by Bernard Rouan.*

left March 1, 1974: Joni performing at the Berkeley Community Theatre. *Photo by Carrie Olson.*

below March 5, 1974: Joni with the jazz guys, Tom Scott and Roger Kellaway of the L.A. Express, in Anaheim, California. *Photo by Matt Gibbons.*

right May 1976: Joni gives up her anonymous traveling identity to preview songs from *Hejira* for some new friends in Alabama. *Photo by Julie Nordmann, from the collection of DiGi and Jet Broughton.*

accessible. "I suspect this will be the most disliked of Miss Mitchell's recordings, despite the fact that it attempts more and makes greater demands on her talent than any of the others. The audience for art songs is far smaller than that for folk ballads, and Joni Mitchell is on the verge of having to make a decision between the two." He couldn't have been more wrong in his characterization of her music. Mitchell had long ago moved away from folk singing. "From the moment I wrote my own songs I was no longer performing folk ballads," she said. "It just was never the right description for what I do as a songwriter. I'm more like Schubert, you know, than a folksinger." The reviewer was also wrong in his prognostication of the popularity of Mitchell's "art songs." Though *Blue* did only reach Number 15 on the *Billboard* chart in 1971, it has gone on to have a remarkably enduring shelf life, the kind of long-term sales that recording and publishing companies dream about. "That record wasn't very popular out of the chute," Joni said. "It was over time that it was discovered. People wore out copies and replaced them and passed them on as gifts and so the numbers ended up getting pretty big on *Blue*."

Later generations of listeners who weren't around to wear out LPs would scratch up *Blue* CDs in ceaseless Discman rotations. The album's hold on listeners is a testament to its major achievement: constructing art from such emotional turmoil. With the immediacy of its musical expression, and its striking lyrical observation, it allows people—especially young people—to insert their own cultural and romantic myths into the songs' narratives. *Blue* has helped many of us come of age without looking away from the confusion of our experience. For some fans of the album, it becomes so much a part of themselves that they feel it is embedded in their DNA. And to be sure, Joni Mitchell does want her work to help people:

> "You know, there was a black woman who came up to me. We were in the green room at the Grammys. I was in the holding pen, so it must have been for *Turbulent Indigo*. Anyway, there were rappers like blackbirds on one side of the room and the white people on the other side, and they were not commingling. Kind of deadly quiet because the rappers were being wary and so the whole room had taken on that tone. And through the door came this brown-skinned hairdresser with bleach-blond hair, and she threw her arms open wide and she went, 'Girl, you make me see pictures in my head! Give me a hug.' She gave me this hug and the whole room began to interact. She was like this icebreaker, you know? The best compliments I've gotten have been from the black community. A black pianist named Henry said that I made raceless, genderless music. I really treasure that he felt that way about it, because that's what I hoped I would do . . .
>
> "There are several movies, *Love Actually* being one and *You've Got Mail* being another . . . in those two movies, guys ask a girl 'Why do you like Joni Mitchell?' I forget what she says in *You've Got Mail*, but he's got another re-

tort and puts me down, kind of like 'What is she getting at, did she take flying lessons?' Their whole relationship becomes estranged because of me, because she doesn't like his boat and he doesn't like her music. Whereas in *Love Actually*, he asks her why she likes Joni Mitchell, and she says, 'She taught your cold English wife how to feel.' I thought that was touching, because that's one of the things that it's trying to do.

"There was this big-hearted bouncer in a bar in Chicago. I walked in and he took one look at me and started to tear up. He said, 'Without you, I never would have understood women.' How was that accomplished, what was the breakthrough line? Sometimes they're funny little things. Like one guy told me the line that got him was 'If you're a friend to me' as opposed to 'friend of mine' [from "For Free"]. The simple distinction—possessing the friend or not—that made it for him. Sometimes you put something down, and a lightbulb goes off in someone's head. You never know exactly what it is that people are getting out of this stuff, or what is the piece they need."

4

Singing the Blues Makes You Bluer

THERE HAVE ALWAYS BEEN CONFLICTING perspectives on the value and purpose of autobiographical writing. Here's how writer Bob Shacochis determines its value:

> When Barry Lopez asked tribal elders in traditional cultures, "What do you mean by a storyteller?" they answered, *When the stories you tell help*. Writing is an essential act of community, no matter that it is born and executed in isola-

tion and self-exile. The point you have to come to is this: *Am I alone after reading this story?* With a great writer, you never touch bottom, and you never feel alone.

If personal songwriting's merit also lies in whether or not it helps the listener, *Blue* has succeeded admirably. *Blue* was Mitchell's first album to ring with personal truth and resound with the power of transformation. It is the sort of record fans have played in part as therapy, cueing up its emotion and riding its cresting and falling waves to something like catharsis. "Before we had Prozac, we had you," Joni says someone once told her, as she likes to repeat.

But it didn't help Joni herself. She remembers the period of *Blue*'s recording as the unhappiest one of her life, a time of "descent." In the studio, her engineer Henry Lewy closed the studio door to all distractions. "We had to lock the door 'cause if somebody came in and looked at me cross-eyed I burst into tears," she told me. "You know, I was weeping all the time." Mitchell said things weren't much better outside the studio.

"I had a year of great sorrow. Or maybe two or three. In that transitional period, I felt transparent and was extremely distraught about many things. I had disturbing nightmares or dreams where all of the problems of the world descended on me. The starving were in my house wearing my clothes . . . I was stranded on the moon and extincted the last flowers up there and God came onto the moon in my dream and got pissed off at me."

Mitchell's nervous intelligence had led her to a crisis of hypersensitivity. Vulnerability wasn't so enchanting when she was living it rather than singing it. So in 1971 she escaped to British Columbia's secluded Sunshine Coast, where she bought some land and started building a small, austere stone house. She was retired, she told her friends, and intended to stay there permanently.

MUCH CRITICAL CONTROVERSY has surrounded the esthetic value of autobiography, but its benefit as catharsis for the writer is usually presumed. It all goes back to autobiographical writing's connection to confession. In 1967, a *Times Literary Supplement* reviewer said of Anne Sexton's *Live or Die*, "many of Mrs. Sexton's new poems are arresting, but such naked psyche-baring makes demands which cannot always be met. Confession may be good for the soul, but absolution is not the poet's job, nor the reader's either." The entry on confessional poetry in *The Oxford Companion to Twentieth-century Poetry in English*, which aspires to an objective didacticism, asserts: "At its worst, Confessional poetry is a kind of therapy that thrusts private experience upon an unwilling reader." This critical analysis stems quite reasonably from the form's history. Anne Sexton's fruitful foray into poetry writing on a suggestion from her analyst became the creative impetus for many less gifted writers who packed shelves with reams of artless poetry in the following decades. But built into the definition is an assumption of confession's therapeutic value. In music, too, an amateur singer pouring her heart out on open mic night is usually assumed to be doing it for her own good, if not for the good of music or those hearing it.

So why didn't the act of unburdening herself on *Blue* help Mitchell? Maybe it did, eventually. But first, why should or shouldn't it help? Autobiographical art doesn't serve its creators, Sylvia Plath once emphatically said, because they must transform feelings for the sake of art into simpler and more concrete sentiments than are true. It certainly didn't provide long-term solace for poets such as Plath, Sexton and Berryman, each of whom eventually committed suicide.

Confession as a soul-cleansing endeavor and means to holiness has been around since Augustine, and the sacrament of penance has been a formal practice in the Catholic Church since 1215, when it was codified by the Lateran Council. As the centuries passed, confession entered the secular realm. Michel Foucault has shown how central confession was for the institutional imposition of rules on minds and bodies. As subjects confess their deviance or crime, they legitimize the institutions set up to regulate them—whether that institution is the justice system or an afternoon talk show. "The obligation to confess," Foucault wrote, "is now relayed through so many different points, is so deeply ingrained in us, that we no longer perceive it as the effect of a power that constrains us; on the contrary, it seems to us that truth, lodged in our most secret nature, 'demands' only to surface; that if it fails to do so, this is because a constraint holds it in place . . . and it can finally be articulated only at the price of a kind of liberation."

Confession as a form of institutional power seeped into popular culture toward the end of the twentieth century, when autobiographical writing came to be applied, in many cases, as a kind of cure. "Journaling" became a verb and was touted by some as successful and cathartic a form of "therapy" as talking to an analyst, and certainly cheaper. Self-help books such as Julia Cameron's high-selling *The Artist's Way*, published in 1992, called for readers to produce something called "the morning pages," a daily practice of writing thoughts without editing to tap into creativity. This practice isn't intended to unveil the writer's multifaceted, innermost feelings through well-crafted prose so much as to strip the self bare in a haste to get to one's most painful and disturbing truths.

By now the idea of writing the self into wellness has been etched into the culture at large. In Stephen Fry's *The Ode Less Travelled: Unlocking the Poet Within*, a populist how-to poetry book published in 2005, the author says we all have secret passions that allow us to wind down and relax—painting, music, gardening. Fry's passion is poetry. He writes, "For me the private act of writing poetry is songwriting, confessional, diary-keeping, speculation, problem-solving, storytelling, therapy, anger management, craftsmanship, relaxation, concentration and spiritual adventure all in one inexpensive package." This somewhat comic conception of poetry as cure-all has sold a lot of books, and it most likely isn't the promise of craftsmanship that entices so many would-be poets to part with their money. What human need is not covered in this list of poetry's functions? In popular culture, writing oneself is a way *out*. Writing as cure trumps writing as craft.

That's the general conception of memoir, anyway. But for Joni Mitchell, personal songwriting was art and craft. It didn't solve any of her problems.

THIS TAINT OF AMATEUR ART as a self-help remedy makes many autobiographical songwriters loath to own up to any therapeutic value for themselves in making music. This is certainly true of Loudon Wainwright III. Loudon is one of America's most enduringly autobiographical songwriters but is not terribly well known, though the recent success of his musician children, Rufus and Martha, has brought him some renown by association. For more than thirty years, he has crafted satirical tunes and nakedly frank songs about forbidden subjects such as abortion (in "That Hospital," he reveals that he and his wife at the time, singer-songwriter Kate McGarrigle, nearly aborted their daughter, Martha) or corporal punishment (in the truly confessional "Hitting You," he addresses the shame of spanking the five-year-old Martha a little too hard when she wouldn't shut up on a car trip). Wainwright explores these taboo subjects with unusual clarity and honesty, but also with a rare and refreshing dose of witty self-deprecation. "I'm like my daddy, I'm just the same," he sings in "Just a John." "He loved to play that cheatin' game." But Wainwright is only playing at the role of blues crooner counting notches on his belt; he goes on to conclude disparagingly that as a "ladies' man" he is an even "bigger fool" than those who "choose booze, smack, or crack" or who "lose it all at the race track."

In 2004, Wainwright gave a brilliantly funny and revealing lecture at Ohio University's Spring Literary Festival. The lecture's title was "My Cool Life: The Singer-Songwriter as Autobiographer," and in it he directly addressed the subject at hand.

> "Frequently I'm asked if writing and singing personal songs is in any way therapeutic. It's true I have had people thank me for writing certain songs, usually ones about the family, the passage of time, and death, three of my absolute favorite topics. I'm certainly always happy to help someone, particularly a paying customer, make it through the night. As to whether what I do is therapeutic for myself, I doubt it. My career has provided me with a living and a half-assed identity, but having it hasn't resolved any of my so-called stuff. I don't think songwriting is curative. In fact, it could be argued that singing the blues in the end just makes you bluer."

Later, in response to a question about whether or not singing songs is therapeutic, Wainwright at first stuck to his claim that it was not. But when pressed, he allowed, "Well, it has benefits. I get paid to do it. A friend of mine who's a pretty good songwriter and a dear friend once wrote some liner notes to a record I made almost thirty years ago. A live record called *A Live One*. My friend wrote in these liner notes, 'What would happen if he didn't wield an ax [guitar], he would be an ax murderer,' that it was a way of venting spleen. And I suppose there's something to be said for that; that I found an outlet. But I don't think it's fixed anything, which is what therapy implies."

When I asked if there wasn't some therapy in clarity alone—in naming and identifying and narrating things—he replied, "Yeah, I think there is," and then said it was the first time he'd admitted that. "Just writing a song about Thanksgiving with your family, maybe that makes it easier the next time you go to Thanksgiving."

Then the conversation took another turn when I asked if writing something confessional ever made him feel worse.

"Yeah," Wainwright said, "I think sometimes it can make you feel worse singing songs over and over about some fucked-up thing. I mean, how could that be good? And maybe it reinforces—you know, in your real life it creates problems. On the other hand, if it's a good song it has to be written, I suppose. But I don't think it solves any neurotic tendencies that I'm aware of. And maybe if dwelling on the subject, if we're talking about the personal songs about dysfunction, whether if it's with the kids or my parents or my father—it hasn't brought us closer together. In fact, it could be argued that it's made things more difficult—with my kids, anyway.

"But when my father died in 1988, that record *History*, which was informed by that experience, really took me into writing about family and the problems. People who like what I do were very affected by that record because it had all happened to them. So that was a good thing. If people are affected by your songs, that is a therapy, too. Because that confirms your own thoughts or feelings or prejudices."

Wainwright kept coming back around to the idea that personal songwriting's value to him was subservient to its value to his listeners and even dependent on that external merit—he humorously and somewhat disingenuously dismissed his need to help listeners as just another component of his need to entertain.

PRIVATE FACES IN PUBLIC PLACES are wiser and nicer, W. H. Auden wrote, than public faces in private places. After she recorded the soul-bearing *Blue*, on which she made her private face most public, Mitchell couldn't shake that image even in her most private moments. It seemed like everyone around Los Angeles knew and recognized her. Mitchell's hypersensitive emotional state combined with her growing fame to make her extremely uncomfortable in most social situations.

"Part of my problem was that I couldn't remember proper nouns so I couldn't remember people's names. *Oh God, there's that person, I've met them ten times and I can't remember their name.* All the storage space for proper nouns had been taken over by ideas. And people would confront me and say, 'I met you ten times and you don't remember my name?' I'd say, 'You've got to forgive me, it's just . . . you can't get blood from a stone.' It was embarrassing and it made me kind of shy. So this social handicap would drive me into isolation; it was making me uncomfortable. If I gave everybody nicknames, I would have been fine. I should have just gone eccentric and given everybody nicknames because I'm not ultimately antisocial."

Joni wasn't so depressed that people could "walk all over her," she said. One problem was friends assuming someone with so much insight in songs would have ready advice for them, too. "You think I'm supposed to be counseling everything to you, why would I?" she'd snarl. "You're completely untrustworthy," she remembers telling even close friends. "You're a narcissist." Even though she worried about her social responsibilities, she felt as an artist she was only obliged to put her empathy into her music.

She soon became wary of everyone. "There's a lot of charlatans, and when you're that down, your jive detector can spot it in an instant," she said. "When you become successful to a degree, you are a magnet for takers. You know, he who piles up treasures draws down thieves [*laughing*]. The whole riding of the rock star thing is not easy. Jimi died, Janis died, Mama Cass died. People died from it."

Assuming she just wasn't cut out for public life, Mitchell left Los Angeles and its stresses for the Sunshine Coast of British Columbia.

"I thought I had the hermit gene. There's one on each side of the family. Uncle Lyall, he lived alone with cats. My uncle Andy went all the way up into the Yukon. So I thought, *OK, I must have the hermit gene. I'm young, I'm in my twenties. I gotta find a place that will replace people, it's got to be intricate and full of change. It's got to be interesting every day.* I looked and looked and looked. Finally, I picked a piece of land."

The land she purchased was on a hidden stretch of Halfmoon Bay, a couple of hours north of Vancouver. The Sunshine Coast itself was only a forty-minute ferry ride from the city, but it felt much more remote. Later in the '70s, the area would gain renown through the *Beachcombers* TV series, which was set in Gibsons Landing, the first town off the ferry. But when Mitchell arrived, it was still largely undiscovered. On the coast, she found resonance with the Sechelt First Nation, an economically and culturally flourishing native "band," as a tribe is known in Canada. Just a few miles from her property was Mount Daniel, a peak of great ceremonial significance to the Sechelt. Rings of stones still marked the peak where native girls had arranged them during puberty rites.

"I learned at an early age to find the beauty of being alive in small, quiet relationship with nature. Sitting quietly. And maybe it's because I have native blood that I'm able to do that or need that, I don't know. But certainly I have a deep respect for native spirituality and culture in general and it feels like part of my being."

On her property was a small derelict cabin where Joni sometimes stayed while she oversaw the building of her home. Joni's old high school friend Tony Simon was one of the few people who visited her there. "The thing had probably been there for one hundred years, we're talking old," he said. The cabin was raised, with a divider separating a ten-by-eight bedroom and small kitchen and bathroom. "She was living in there, painting and writing and leading a creative life. I remember being quite impressed because she was doing things and living in very tough conditions. Maybe she was beating herself up with tough conditions, I don't know." Joni did bring a certain asceticism to the house she built, which she has described as "almost like a monastery. All stone and hardwood floors and hardwood benches, everything that would be corrective. No mirrors. Fighting for all that good virtue in myself.

When I left my house in Laurel Canyon, I looked around and it seemed too soft, too comfortable, too dimly lit, too much red upholstery . . . I just made this place really uncomfortable, like a corrective shoe."

Artists have long retreated from the mundane and complex demands of urban life to Spartan rural sanctuaries where they can restore creative purity. The jazz world, for example, calls this tradition woodshedding. After hearing John Coltrane's leaps of innovation in 1959, an intimidated Sonny Rollins exiled himself from the jazz scene, using the Williamsburg Bridge as an open-air practice room. Rollins didn't return to performance and recording until he felt he could again live up to his title of tenor saxophone titan.

For her part, Mitchell wasn't contending with competition when she left the industry. She had exceeded all other songwriters in lyrical intimacy and surpassed most others in musical complexity. In retrospect, Mitchell says her post-*Blue* crisis was the product of achieving sudden fame while still burdened with the shame of having given up a daughter for adoption in 1965.

"I lost my child in '65, I had no money, I couldn't take her. I had no roof over my head. I was destitute. My talent hadn't come in—I hadn't begun to write. Three years later, I had enough money to buy a house and a car. So there's always the question, *How could I have held on to her for those three years?* So anyway, needless to say, there's a hole in you, like you've lost a piece of you. It isn't with you twenty-four hours a day, but it's kind of a nagging thing. So that was my deep dark hidden secret. And I protected it from my parents and . . . although I'm a Scorpio and I'm supposed to be secretive by nature, something happened along the line, around the time of *Blue*, where my secretive nature basically exploded or imploded or whatever."

It was probably both—her sorrow probably imploded within her while exploding into the songs of *Blue*, which were honest about everything *but* her daughter. When Mitchell finally was reunited with her daughter, Kilauren Gibb, in 1997, fans were quick to cite their long separation as cause for Mitchell's enigmatic and temperamental persona. She supported this interpretation, saying that music had been nothing more than a way to fill the painful void of childlessness and maintained that her creative muse departed upon the reunion with Gibb. That didn't last, as in 2006 Mitchell began to experience one of the most productive periods of her career.

Joni has often depicted her twenty-two-year-old pregnant self as a sexual innocent lost in a harsh and judgmental society that ostracized single mothers. In a rare recording of Joni performing six months pregnant at Toronto's Half Beat Club in October 1964, Mitchell does sound naïve and lonely. She covers Woody Guthrie's "Pastures of Plenty," "Every Night When the Sun Goes Down," a traditional song, and a version of Sydney Carter's "Crow on the Cradle" that is particularly affecting when you consider her plight at the time. Still, it's her sanguine voice that grabs you. There's no loss in it. She's not yet had to give up anything. No matter how bleak the folk ballads' lyrics may be, her voice bears none of the characteristic disillusionment that would shade her music from her first professional recording on.

In video footage of Mitchell performing soon after giving birth, she exhibits extraordinary poise for someone with so little stage experience, and the strong drive of someone on the way up. As difficult as giving up her daughter may have been, Mitchell had been around enough to see that building a musical career is demanding work. Throughout the second half of the '60s, she toured without break, toiling in small clubs on the folk circuit and painstakingly making a name for herself as a songwriter and performer. She didn't stop constant touring or traveling until just before recording *Blue*. Performing gives many singers a reliable rush and many have testified that it also takes them out of themselves for a few hours. Perhaps Mitchell's "descent" after the release of *Blue* had something to do with her no longer benefiting from the catharsis of stage performance. Perhaps it was the first time in six years she'd stopped long enough to take a look at herself, to consider where she'd been and where she was going. After all, in that time she had progressed from an anonymity in Saskatoon to being the queen of Laurel Canyon, heart of the singer-songwriter scene.

The most telling thing in an artist's life is often the art

itself. "The best of my mind all goes down on the strings and the page," Mitchell would later admit on *Don Juan's Reckless Daughter*. During her time in Halfmoon Bay, ostensibly a retirement from the industry, Mitchell didn't stop working. She wrote the songs for *For the Roses*, which was released in 1972. A photograph on the album cover shows Mitchell sitting on a mossy bank on her Halfmoon Bay property, camouflaged in green velvet and brown leather boots, very much at home in nature. She gets even more natural in the inside photograph, which is a nude shot from behind. She stands alone on a rock in the water off the coast. Years later she explains:

> *"Blue* had been all I could write at that time. As a result it's pure and it's empowered, and there's no artifice in it. I was stripped naked, you know? So I put myself naked on my next album cover symbolically. Not as an exhibitionist, really, because that's what I did—I came up, dropped out in the bush where there was nobody and ran around naked. My own private Eden."

The iconography is clear. Mitchell had laid herself bare on *Blue*, and would do the same on *For the Roses:* "The next album was still intimate, although it didn't garner the same attention—as a matter of fact, I think in some ways it's more intimate than *Blue*."

Once Mitchell escaped Los Angeles and the music industry, she couldn't seem to stop thinking about it. Many of *For the Roses'* songs take on the industry's vacuous greed and her own ambivalence about her flourishing position within it. She also devotes much lyrical attention to the industry's seduction and pitfalls for colleagues like James Taylor, with whom she had a short, intense affair in late 1970 and early 1971 before heading out for Canada. In February 1970, Taylor had released his second album, *Sweet Baby James*, and the success of its first single, "Fire and Rain," established him as both a performer and songwriter. The first songs Taylor had played on guitar were the hymns and carols from the Protestant hymnal at his Massachusetts boarding school, Milton Academy, and he constructed his fingerpicking technique around their harmonic structure. The hymn's simple formula of calming inspiration lingered on in his music, giving soothing ballast to the bleak confessional lyrics of songs like "Fire and Rain," which addressed Taylor's time in a mental institution and the suicide of a friend. "I've seen lonely times when I could not find a friend / But I always thought I'd see you again." Taylor's music offered an attractive balance: his most hopeless lyrics were buoyed by gospel chords and by something more ineffable—an inborn entitlement to the good life due to his upbringing in a patrician family; on the other hand, his songs about rainbows and Carolina sunshine had the counterweight of psychological gloom. He'd committed himself as a psychiatric patient at McLean Hospital, which gave his fans plenty of dark mystery on which to speculate.

Taylor's air of troubled nobility complemented his good looks, which carried the kindly appeal of a cool uncle. "He had a very elegant way of suffering," Joni told me. Less piercing and esoteric than songwriters like Leonard Cohen or Mitchell, Taylor became wildly successful in 1970 and established the definitive folk-oriented soft-rock style emulated by many in the following years. But this instant celebrity after *Sweet Baby James* exacerbated an ongoing struggle with heroin addiction to create an imperfect storm of personal crisis for Taylor, which was his state when Joni Mitchell fell in love with him. When James played guitar on *Blue*, he was no help in her time of distress, she said: "James was a walking psychological disaster anyway. He'd been institutionalized and butted cigarettes on his arm, you know? He was not in any position to point a finger."

On *For the Roses*, Mitchell wrote about the difficulty of "hold[ing] the hand of a rock 'n' roll man" in "Blonde in the Bleachers." She wrote about Taylor's heroin addiction in "Cold Blue Steel and Sweet Fire." When Taylor released his third album, *Mud Slide Slim and the Blue Horizon* in April 1971, the enormity of his success caused critics to condemn him. Mitchell addresses celebrity's backlash in her title track: "Just when you're getting a taste for worship / They start bringing out the hammers / And the boards / And the nails." The most autobiographical portrait of her relationship with Taylor comes in "See You Sometime." The song's narrator wonders if he's in some hotel room, with a view. Or caught in a crowd, or "holding some honey who came on to you?" If there's any doubt whom she's addressing, she references Taylor's attire in the cover photograph of the *Mud Slide Slim* album: "Pack your suspenders, I'll come meet your plane." On *For the Roses*, Mitchell also continued to expose rarely discussed romantic dilemmas, like an inability to hang with her lover's friends. "Oh baby I can't seem to make it with you socially," she sings. It's unsurprising that Mitchell would mine such a short-lived romance for so much lyrical material, as she had previously extracted more than a few lines from her fling with Leonard Cohen.

Alone on the Sunshine Coast, Mitchell certainly had ample time to mull over her relationship with Taylor. As she stayed on there, friends back in Los Angeles worried she might be having a nervous breakdown. Most concerning was the news that she was trying to give up smoking. "That definitely helped make it the worst year of my life!" Joni said. More seriously, she went on: "If I'd been born into a tradition that had shamans in it, we would have recognized that the symptoms I was going through were the coming in of shamanic powers." But she was born into a tradition that handled such symptoms with psychiatry.

"I went to a couple of shrinks and went, 'Whoa, you're dangerous.' There was nothing wrong with me clinically. I wasn't a manic anything. The first shrink just said, 'You can't shrink a genius.' And I might add, 'Or an Irish person.' Certainly, I'm unshrinkable. So I picked another shrink that didn't believe in psychiatry. I went to him and wept for a couple of weeks and got a boyfriend and he went, 'OK, get out of here, you're cured, all you needed was someone to talk to.' And that was the truth, that's a good shrink."

The boyfriend to whom she unburdened herself was Tony Simon. Though they'd long been nothing more than good friends, they became intimate when he took a girlfriend to the Sunshine Coast. Joni was alone at the time, and staying at Lord Jim's Lodge, just down the road from her property. "We all went to dinner and drank like it was going out of style," Simon said. "I've used the word *competitive* with Joni. She decided that she was going to outlast this girl and she was gonna sleep with me that night. And that's what ended up happening." Simon and Mitchell spent the night in her room at Lord Jim's—after pouring his smashed girlfriend into the van, where she woke up alone the next morning.

Of course, "free love" meant very different things for men and women. Joni realized that, quite painfully, when *Rolling Stone* made its list of her romantic conquests.

"Our generation was more experimental and they were going 'free love, free love.' Well, there was no such thing, it was a big ruse. Nobody knows that better than me, because I got taken out in the summer of love and a list was drawn of all the hearts theoretically that I had broken. And on this list was every man whose radio show I did, they're assuming that I'm screwing every man that comes in contact with me and even some on the list that I never even met. That's what the song 'Blue' was about. 'You know I've been to sea before'—I was in love with Graham Nash, and had written about it, so everyone knew . . . 'crown and anchor me' is a metaphor for the actual situation for women at the time. You were supposed to be tied down."

But Mitchell had always been more practical than moral about sex.

"There's one thing I've understood since my early twenties, which was miniskirt period. So many girls were getting their bottoms pinched because they were wearing a short skirt that fit like a bathing suit. And they're complaining. And I'd say, 'Don't you understand anything about men?' I keep the company of men. I'm privy to locker room talk . . . they're easily stimulated. So if you know that about their apparatus, do you have to passively seduce everybody? Save that for your boyfriend."

Joni seemed to find a solution in playing the part of the aggressor in romance. "She dealt with sexual situations as if she were a guy," Simon said. "I'm not aware of anybody seducing her. It was always her choice. She was always able to have sex and then decide if they were relationship-worthy later." For several months, Simon and Mitchell saw each other nonexclusively. "In a way, Tony spoiled me for a relationship because he gave me a lot of liberty," Joni said. "We did a lot of things together, but we were not girlfriend and boyfriend. We never went steady or put any romantic claims on it, we just enjoyed each other. And it gave me an appetite for that kind of relationship with men, which I found easier because they're more up for mischief [*laughs*]."

After she and Simon decided they were not meant for a real relationship—mutually, without discussion—Mitchell remained friends with him, as was usually the case with her ex-lovers. Neither of them felt jilted. Simon soon called to invite her down to a "really neat" place in Mexico where he was staying. The transition to friendship was not always so easy, as Joni's lyrical obsession with James Taylor on *For the Roses* makes clear. But her relationship with Simon was typical of the serial romantic life she would practice throughout the '70s.

In her Halfmoon Bay hermitage, Mitchell was establishing another pattern that would define most of her adult life. She began to develop her ability to be alone into an artistic strategy. Stewing over James Taylor in solitude had a very central purpose to her work, as Tony Simon began to notice at the time. Here he's looking back on decades of close friendship with her.

"She has not only spent a lot of time alone, but she's spent a lot of time in introspection. When she does that, I think it creates a disconnect from reality in some way. Something minor happens—in an affair or let's just say even

missing a day of school in grade twelve—but if she thinks
and thinks and thinks about it, then she somehow ends up
making it important. Because she spends a long time alone,
not letting things out, the way you do in normal social in-
teraction or, say, in a long-term commitment, these things
inside her start getting mixed up. Not in terms of confusion, exactly, but mixed like a soup, mixed in with all these
other experiences. And the minor thing begins to take on
a bigger meaning than it ever really had, a dramatization,
maybe. In many ways her creativity *springs* from all that.
So she's deliberately sacrificing a certain element of being
like others and living like others. And she's sacrificing that
to her creative urge."

Joni may have had a genuine conflict between love and
freedom, but she came to cultivate deliberately that conflict
for the purposes of her art. A lifestyle of serial romanticism allowed her to experience an affair's stream of small episodes and
feelings, which would be followed by the stillness of solitude,
when she could then worry those passing events into the big
themes of her songs. This made for some of the most memorable records of her Blue Period: *Blue*, *For the Roses*, *Court and
Spark*, *Hejira*. It also set her up for a life of dissatisfaction. "She
doesn't want to stay married or committed to someone," Tony
said. "She'll always put herself into a position where she can
be alone to rethink things and somehow use them. That's the
nature of the artist. She'll never be satisfied, I hope."

*   *   *

ON *FOR THE ROSES*, Mitchell stretched her lyrics out into more impressionistic lines connected by associative logic:

> *Some get the gravy*
> *And some get the gristle*
> *Some get the marrow bone*
> *And some get nothing*
> *Though there's plenty to spare*
>
> *I took my share down by the sea*
> *Paper plates and Javex bottles on the tide*
> *Seagulls come down and they squawk at me*
> *Down where the water skiers glide*

The critic David Yezzi has analyzed poets' use of associative logic to supplant reason with emotion. He cites bridges of wordplay tenuously linking thoughts in W. D. Snodgrass's "Heart's Needle," for example: "Assuredly your father's crimes / are visited / on you. You visit me sometimes. / The time's up." Such associations suggest that in the grip of emotional honesty, the poem's speaker can no longer think straight, nor does he want to. Similarly, Mitchell admits that her mind is buckling under strain in "Lesson in Survival," also on *For the Roses*. She sings that she went to see a friend, and rambled on to him, revealing "suspicious reasoning." She burns out right there before him, and watches the things she tells him "buckle up in his brow."

Like its lyrics, *For the Roses'* music rambles through line after line without returning to a fixed point or riff. When the songs do have choruses, they fail to stand out from the verses. The accessible melodic hooks of *Blue* are replaced with variable music evincing highly personal feeling. *For the Roses* is a transitional recording, with certain features of her later music: there are multipart instrumental arrangements incorporating winds and percussion, strong jazz inflections (notably Tom Scott's solos on "Cold Blue Steel and Sweet Fire" and "Barangrill"), ambitious formal innovations (e.g., the episodic "Blonde in the Bleachers" and the complicated interludes in "Let the Wind Carry Me" and "Judgement of the Moon and Stars [Ludwig's Tune]"), and a new polish in vocal performance.

For the Roses' expanded musical scope can be heard as an expression of Mitchell reaching back to her childhood, when she lived serenely under the changing weather of the Saskatchewan prairies. In "Let the Wind Carry Me," for example, she tries to make sense of her father's and mother's respective tolerance and condemnation of her teenage rebellion, and to find a middle way between them. But Mitchell doesn't recover her childhood equanimity here, nor does her music manage to open up to the immensity of the Canadian prairies. She is still constrained by doubts about the negative aspects of her character. Equanimity would only come later, on the 1976 *Hejira*, when Mitchell, informed by Buddhist philosophy, embraced and celebrated the duality of her own character. What Mitchell did repossess as she worked on *For the Roses* in Halfmoon Bay was the secret of her joy, as she told Vic Garbarini in 1983:

> "One day about a year after I started my retreat in Canada, I went out swimming. I jumped off a rock into this dark emerald green water with yellow kelp in it and purple starfish at the bottom. It was very beautiful, and as I broke up to the surface of the water, which was black and reflective, I started laughing. Joy had just suddenly come over me, you know? And I remember that as a turning point. First feeling like a loony because I was out there laughing all by myself in this beautiful environment [*laughs*]. And then, right on top of it, was the realization that whatever my social burdens were, my inner happiness was still intact."

This description seems the product of great poetic license, but my summertime visits to Halfmoon Bay confirmed that the colors of its marine life really are the stuff of a psychedelic Beatles cartoon—she failed to mention the bay's busy population of brown seals that skim the surface of the dark green water like dim memories. This account, which places heavy emphasis on a defining event, shows another of Mitchell's conversion moments. Her sorrows weren't over, but the following years did prove she had found a place in which she could continually fulfill her own directive to "get back to the garden."

Over the decades, she would travel to the stone house in British Columbia about twice a year.

The autobiographical *Blue* initially created more crisis than cure in Mitchell. Singing about herself so frankly put her in a position where things had to get worse before they got better. She went into self-imposed exile for a year, and when it was over, she had created a safe haven where she could perpetually recover her sense of well-being and reenact the fantasy of confronting natural rather than man-made trials. Mitchell told me that the Sunshine Coast retreat is the place she feels most comfortable and secure. She often mentions that it's where she can smoke as much as she wants, which is another way of saying she feels free from harsh judgment there, both her own and others'. She finds self-reflection a gentler pursuit up in Canada.

In September 1971, Mitchell came out of hiding for a surprise guest performance with David Crosby and Graham Nash at the Queen Elizabeth Theatre in Vancouver. Finally, after a year of solitude, it emerged that her "hermit gene" wasn't her defining influence, after all. Soon after the performance, she returned to Los Angeles, in part because she felt the pull of civilization, though there were also a couple of practical reasons. With its expanding orchestration, her music was evolving needs beyond her own accompaniment. Back in Los Angeles, she could work with a band. And she quickly realized her fairytale home on the Sunshine Coast was only a summer cottage. "I wouldn't have gone back to LA except that my house isn't winterized. I had spent one winter in it, but it was four pairs of socks and five shawls, you know. With a generator there's power outages, and when the power goes off, the house freezes up. The house doesn't have storm windows; I have shutters here. It's very close to the water . . . it's *in* the water in the winter."

So Mitchell returned to California and temporarily moved in with David Geffen, proprietor of her new label, Asylum. In early 1972, she headed out on a four-month tour with singer-songwriter Jackson Browne as her opening act. Fans noticed a new womanly definition in her face, her cheekbones more prominent, hair a little shorter, voice a bit deeper. The year away had changed her.

5

Beyond Personal Songwriting

IN COLLEGE I WENT ON A CAMPING TRIP in Colorado's Rocky Mountain National Park with my boyfriend, Steve, and his father, Jim. At each campground, Jim's routine was the same. He would carefully pitch his tent, spread out his sleeping bag, and cue up a Dan Fogelberg tape on his boom box. Then he'd lay back with his hands linked under his head and gaze out dreamily through the tent's netting into the pine-scented upper altitude, with Fogelberg providing the soundtrack to his vacation bliss. Though it seemed unsympathetic to disparage the industrious man—he'd been editing and publishing a weekly small-town newspaper for forty years—for his vacation pleasures, I was offended by Jim's tranquilizing use of music. At the time, I was most interested in free jazz, which required an active engagement for understanding, and often a masochist's tolerance of the disquietingly raucous. Dan Fogelberg soothed; free jazz unsettled. That, I knew, with the conviction of an avant-garde Nazi, was what art was supposed to do. More than anything, I was embarrassed that Jim, a man whom I admired, would find in Fogelberg's lackluster music and lyrics a profundity that provided an aural equivalent to the grandiose natural setting of the Rockies. When I couldn't stand any more of Fogelberg's mellowness, I'd politely storm away from the campgrounds on steep, punishing hikes up the nearest slopes.

JONI MITCHELL HELPED make personal songwriting the defining literary movement of the late '60s and early '70s, as significant as Beat literature had been a decade earlier. Joni told me that accomplishment was due to her operating beliefs about what a songwriter could and should do.

> "I always thought the duty of a songwriter is the same as
> a duty of a poet. It's to teach people how to view things,
> how to look at things. I remember traveling through Japan
> with a twenty-one-piece entourage and some of the musi-

cians' wives appeared. We were traveling on this fast train and I was shooting photos out the windows. I heard one of them say, 'What's she shooting? What's she seeing?' I heard another one say, 'Well, she doesn't see like we do.' And I thought, *Well, maybe not, but try and look at it this way with me.*"

But when Joni returned to Los Angeles in 1972 from her year of self-imposed exile, the original perspective of autobiographical songs was changing—Bob's, Leonard's, and Joni's ambitious song poetry was becoming a thing of the past. Her new roommate, David Geffen, was signing a number of personal songwriters to his new artist-friendly Asylum Records. Her 1972 *For the Roses* album included a hit single with a light country feel, "You Turn Me On, I'm a Radio," which Mitchell wrote as a smartass response to Geffen's request for a radio-friendly song. She figured lines like "Call me at the station / The lines are open" would appeal to the vanity of deejays, and the single did reach Number 25, becoming Mitchell's first Top 40 hit that she both wrote and recorded. Her other more trenchant critiques of the music industry on *For the Roses* were proving prophetic: Geffen's Asylum artists such as Dan Fogelberg, the Eagles, which originally formed as a back-up band for Linda Ronstadt, and even Jackson Browne would all share a mellower sound and offer up lyrics that pacified rather than probed or questioned. These easy answers were played to smoother tunes with a country inflection, the hint of a hoedown providing a warm authenticity that relieved the lyrics themselves of the burden of being warm or authentic. The new thing was provisional. Affirming minor truths was in. Aspiring to larger ones was, for the most part, out.

In Fogelberg's work, he anointed himself ultrasensitive, graced with the burden of feeling more deeply than the rest of us—forever immortalizing his music in middle-school band rooms, where thirteen-year-old piano or tuba players would two decades later still bleat out Fogelberg's tunes with pained sensitivity. In "Leader of the Band," for example, one of his most successful songs, Fogelberg paid tribute to his bandleader father in tuneful platitudes. After identifying his father as a "cabinet-maker's son" whose hands "were made for different work," a conflation of his dad with none other than Jesus, Fogelberg goes on to describe his father's life as a bandleader, singing that his own "life has been a poor attempt / To imitate the man," that he's "just a living legacy / to the leader of the band."

I'm sure I don't have to go further for fans of good songwriting, but I'm on a roll. Here's the trouble, for me, anyway. "Leader of the Band" celebrates paternal idolatry with a single-mindedness that most children don't feel past the age of six. It's a song of half-truths: at the time of its recording, Fogelberg was a rock star living it up on the road and at home on his high-altitude Colorado ranch. Surely, he had aspired to something other than the achievements, however admirable, of his local Illinois bandleader father? Fogelberg's confidence in loving clichés seems a defense against the harsh realities of familial relationships rather than an examination of them. For anyone with mixed feelings about his or her father, which includes just about everyone, Fogelberg's optimism for simple truths may even produce feelings of inadequacy.

This is admittedly dangerous territory. Who am I to suggest what should or should not strike a universal chord for music fans? I am merely suggesting that as personal songwriting became popular and reached more people, it faltered, for many reasons. "In 1972, it looked as though the singer-songwriter movement might coalesce into a broad-based adult tradition as vital and long-lived as the craftsmanly lineage of Jerome Kern, Irving Berlin, Cole Porter, Rodgers and Hart, and the Gershwins," wrote critic Stephen Holden in his study of the tradition. "One envisaged writers like Paul Simon, Joni Mitchell, Randy Newman, James Taylor and Jackson Browne turning out recorded song cycles with the same regularity that their Broadway and Tin Pan Alley antecedents created theater and movie scores. But instead of solidifying and taking over pop, the movement disintegrated."

One of the reasons for the demise of autobiographical songwriting was a dearth of new talent to match the old. Dan Fogelberg's work is a far cry from the potent complexity of emotion Dylan had inaugurated in song just a decade before. And it's worlds apart, for example, from Joni Mitchell's songs like "For the Roses," on which she was willing to implicate herself in her own problems. There she sang that she must seem ungrateful, her "teeth sunk in the hand" of the industry that brings her things she couldn't give up just yet. Mitchell deconstructs familiar arguments and easy solutions, using displacement to mark her mind's defense mechanisms. Both Dylan and Mitchell were willing to leave listeners with the discomfort of irresolution. Later songwriters like Fogelberg seemed to need to reassure their listeners, and possibly themselves.

Along with the dilution of astringent human observation into the commonplaces of the new country-rock acts, another songwriting trend emerged in Mitchell's wake, perhaps best exemplified by Carly Simon. Simon was a voluptuous singer-songwriter—her bombshell sex appeal was her artistic banner—with poetic aspirations whose high-profile affair with Warren Beatty and marriage to James Taylor lent interest to her depictions of romance, especially when it went wrong. But songs such as "You're So Vain," for all its humor, was content to vilify her lover and showed an unwillingness to accept a fundamental share of the blame for trouble in affairs of the heart, placing her instead in the position of romantic victim. In addition to this lack of personal accountability, there was little of the investigation that turns over relationship woes for insights into human behavior. Mitchell was a great songwriter whose natural beauty helped advance her career. Like many of the female songwriters who followed, Carly Simon was incredibly photogenic, but her melodies and lyrics were dim picture negatives of more artful songwriting. In much simpler language than Simon, Leonard Cohen managed to own up to his part in the complications of romance. He admitted to less than noble intentions in "Hallelujah": he did his best, though "it wasn't much"; he couldn't feel, so he "tried to touch."

The well-wrought songs of Leonard Cohen or certain ones of James Taylor had a sensitizing effect on listeners. Some songwriters assumed that effect as an affectation, over-emoting and using songs to smear audiences with extremes of feeling. John Lennon's first full-fledged solo album, in which he expelled anger in a scathingly honest autobiographical work inspired by his and Yoko Ono's primal scream therapy, is an extreme example. But as the '70s progressed, even singers less vested in catharsis and compulsion would perform histrionics with little concern for control and craft. The difference between earlier autobiographical songs and later ones is something like the difference between a piece of writing that evokes a "small sob in the spine of the reader," which is how Nabokov once described his writing aim, and a journal entry that vents feelings.

Larger cultural forces may have been at work in songwriting's turn from bracing self-reflection to fainthearted solipsism. Early singer-songwriters lamented an ephemeral dream, the baby boom counterculture's utopian ideals. Bob Dylan's disillusionment with the principles of the '60s led him to look at his own emotional vicissitudes instead. It was as if Dylan arrived at the same rationale in using the first person that Thoreau had when he defended his use of "I" in the introduction to *Walden:* even when we discuss high concepts, we're all talking about ourselves anyway, right? Dylan and other singer-songwriters then brought the country's pervasive mood of disenchantment into a pop music that addressed more personal concerns.

Perhaps a songwriting movement founded on the loss of something—in this case, collective ideals—just wasn't going to last, but the decline in the quality of autobiographical songwriting throughout the 1970s also had something to do with a lack of craftsmanship and honesty. While Dylan in the mid- to late '60s evoked a mood of disenchantment through frank, mind-jarring, impressionistic images, the self-involved songwriters who followed merely inhabited moods of disenchantment. Even when they sang in the first person, Mitchell, with her musical drive, and Dylan, with his poetic zeal, almost always aspired to illuminate larger human truths. As Carly Simon's accusatory and self-justifying second-person "You're So Vain" showed, it's not only the first-person voice that can emanate from egoism. Even singer-songwriter Billy Joel had his doubts about the merits of personal songwriting: "Without naming names, I don't necessarily buy that a confessional school of songwriting makes for more integrity. It's always 'We're seeing him progress as a person.' I think it's better to progress on a record as a musician."

There was a certain irony in autobiographical songwriters' successes. Early songwriters expressed private concerns and were mindful of audience's expectations for intimacy. Mitchell once told Alice Echols that she originally became a "confessional poet" because "I thought, *You'd better know who you're applauding up here*. It was a compulsion to be honest with my audience." Echols noted that as Joni's audience grew, "baring her soul no longer narrowed the gap between performer and audience; it was, after all the source of her celebrity." James Taylor also first played to small clubs of reflective listeners who saw and heard their concerns mirrored by a lone, exposed figure in a musical soliloquy. Then he became popular. As the *Rolling Stone* review of Taylor's 1971 *Mud Slide Slim and the Blue Horizon* noted, "The Rolling Stones in their flamboyance can excite mass appeal; when James does, something has gone askew. James' career is the lie to his art, for, if he is by nature an introspective reclusive, the effect of his career is the opposite." Taylor became aware of the irony as early as the time of that recording, which was filled with apologetics for his touring life on the road and with reflections about what it was like to be a reflective songwriter. But as the reviewer went on to assess, "James himself perpetuates his problems, by releasing a best-selling record which aims at their solution." Many songwriters who followed were less self-aware: when Dan Fogelberg later sang to thousands of adoring fans that he was nothing more than his small-town bandleader father's son, the incongruity of the message and his rock star presentation went unacknowledged. The sentiment rang hollow. Joni told me she never adapted to larger stages: "I always felt too small up there. What's to look at? Pink Floyd always had some kind of extravaganza, they knew they were standing there inactively. What's to look at? That's how I always felt. Not on a small stage, when you're doing work that suits a small room, and you can also kid around. The pressure is different. But the big stage, I never felt adequate on it."

In November 1976, Martin Scorsese filmed the historic concert *The Last Waltz*, featuring Bob Dylan's 1966 and 1974 backup group the Band along with an all-star cast that included Dylan, Van Morrison, Joni Mitchell, and Neil Young. It was a musical celebration as well as the Band's final performance. But as Scorsese impatiently noted in a recent interview, "*The Last Waltz* had the word 'last' in it. In a way it's an elegy." An elegy to an era, and to a certain kind of songwriting. The performers all came together at the concert's end to sing Dylan's apocalyptic gospel "I Shall Be Released."

The reemergence of autobiographical songwriters in the '90s especially bothered Joni. "There are lots of imitators of *Blue*," she told me. Joni's Blue Period can be heard in the work of many younger performers, from Tori Amos to Sheryl Crow, Sarah McLachlan to Jane Siberry (or "Issa," as she came to call herself). The way Joni saw it, what passed for self-assurance or political observation in later autobiographical songwriting was actually a lack of maturity, an "I'll show you" sentiment.

> "I got invited to play at this Hollywood soiree where they were giving out awards to movie stars who had done something socially conscious. So I'm the party favorite. Afterward a guy comes up to me and says, 'We could have had Alanis Morissette, you know, but we chose you.' And

I went 'Oh' you know, like I'm supposed to be honored? I didn't say that but I thought, you know, Alanis Morissette is not my favorite playwright, you know . . . girl meets boy, gives him head in the back of the theater and he dumps her and she turns savage and she rummages through his drawers. I don't think she's a great new modern woman. She's just a preacher's brat in rebellion trying to shock Daddy like Madonna. I don't see her as a great thinker, a great woman, a great anything."

ONE WAY BEYOND THE LIMITS of personal songwriting was through the older theatrical tradition of Tin Pan Alley, telling stories and creating dramatic monologues sung by invented characters. Randy Newman sustained a long career this way. Another course of reinvention was to recast autobiography in a different sound: Paul Simon would bring his songwriting new life with the exotic harmonies and rhythms of world music. Joni Mitchell used both strategies.

After the deeply autobiographical *For the Roses*, Mitchell was ready for a change. Early singer-songwriters created an aura of authentic directness by appearing as solo acts with piano or guitar accompaniment. That they were all alone up there made it easier to believe they were testifying truth. For Mitchell, this spare mode of presentation had combined with her disarmingly candid lyrics to create an image of a vulnerable blonde. On tour with Jackson Browne in 1972, she saw that her delicate performances were associated with her own pain, loss, and heartbreak—and invited continuous speculation about the identity of her boyfriends. And she was frustrated to observe that, by contrast, no matter how private his material, Browne was seen as being separate from his songs and given the leverage of artistic transformation. Besides, Joni found Jackson's sensitivity to be a ruse: "Jackson Browne is a mini-talent and he's also a phony. And a seducer. 'Looking for a lover that won't blow my cover, she's so hard to find'—that's about the only honest thing that Jackson has ever revealed about himself. His whole thing is to make himself look sensitive and charitable." It should be noted that Joni's romance with Jackson ended badly, so she may have a personal ax to grind.

"I don't want to be vulnerable," she said, with characteristic straightforwardness, to her friend Malka Marom in an interview at the time. She wanted power, and she wanted to share the stage with other musicians who might "absorb some of the loneliness." "I just couldn't stay in that lonely *Blue* place very long," Joni told me. She wanted a band. She wanted to become one of the boys again. Her early tomboy predilections had evolved into a lifelong preference for the company of men.

"I've always been a girl at home in a guy's world. I remember feeling sad—like a cat among dogs—only twice. Only two times when I was in the company of men did I feel I wasn't quite a man. Once in the middle of a recording session where the humor got very scatological. And

I would just be left out. It was too vulgar . . . I couldn't really participate. And the other time was in the middle of a pool game. I'm a good pool player, but you don't dare play that well as a woman. You'll bruise the fun if you play too good. But only two times of discomfort is not bad for a lifelong tomboy."

With its expanding arrangements, Mitchell's music was developing needs beyond her own accompaniment anyway. So it was both a personal and artistic solution when she put together a progressive jazz-rock band. Tom Scott had played woodwinds and reeds on *For the Roses*, but his entire group, the L.A. Express, was recruited for Joni's tour supporting the 1974 *Court and Spark*. The group was known for a synthesis of folk, pop rock, and jazz of the smooth, lounge-lizard variety.

Just before Christmas 1973, Asylum released *Court and Spark*'s first single, "Raised on Robbery," to announce Mitchell's rebirth as a new artist. The hard-rocking song has a radically different sound than her previous work and is built around a story of a prostitute who tries to pick up a man but loses him by trying too hard. (Mitchell said Faye Dunaway once told her, "You're so lucky because you can invent your own roles.") The story, a monologue sung by an imagined character, did as much to distance Mitchell from the song as her rousing backing band did. In "Raised on Robbery" Mitchell also used the studio as an instrument for the first time. Her multitracked vocals, which recall the Andrews Sisters, are contrasted by Robbie

Robertson's electric guitar—Mitchell used none other than Bob Dylan's guitarist in her project to separate her personal identity from her music and become one of the boys.

In January 1974, the complete *Court and Spark* album was released to wide critical and popular acclaim. The record had a pop sound that didn't compromise Mitchell's artistic ideals, because her art had made headway, too: for the first time her arranging skills and vocal confidence were fully incorporated into her songwriting. The songs were connected with interludes, as they are in Richard Strauss's classical song cycles, and images and symbols were repeated, as in a short story collection. Mitchell's first real effort at serious orchestral arrangements and a jazz-oriented sound made for a rich and sophisticated album with appealing lightness. *Court and Spark* could have been the soundtrack to a 1970s Los Angeles dinner party hosted by Joan Didion.

In addition to the prostitute in "Raised on Robbery," Mitchell assumed other characters on the album. "Free Man in Paris" depicted David Geffen's desire to escape his record industry mogul responsibilities, with a cunning and deliberately corny use of the country-rock sound he'd branded on Asylum Records. She concluded the album with her first recording of a song she didn't write, Lambert, Hendricks, and Ross's "Twisted." On it, Mitchell branched out into jazz vocals that reveled in the song's playful first-person account of schizophrenia. Her distance from the song helped make it the best vocal performance of her career up to that point.

Mitchell balanced these outward-looking songs with songs that looked inward as much as any of her earlier work had. Yet even these introspective songs were delivered with a new wit and cleverness through Mitchell's jazz inflection, which both stylized and deepened her admissions. Jazz admits feeling through nonverbal expression. A Lester Young saxophone solo speaks volumes, and Billie Holiday made every song autobiographical through the sheer eloquence of her always-just-about-to-break voice. Jazz soloists make listeners feel like they're talking directly to them. On *Court and Spark*, Mitchell composed this technique into songs like "Down to You," which is about self-reliance in the lonely space between lovers. The vocals are supple, but Mitchell alternates singing lines with others that speak to the listener directly. After singing "Down to you, constant stranger," she then told the listener, "You're a brute, you're an angel, you can crawl, you can fly, too." These speech-like lyrics recall the colloquial strategies of Pablo Neruda, Elizabeth Bishop, and other poets. Mitchell accomplished the additional feat of making these conversational lines as musical as any of the ones that she sings. "Joni Mitchell's unique rhythmic approach to melodies has to do, for me, with a total conversational ease," the jazz pianist Brad Mehldau wrote. "A wonderful feeling of casualness that makes the music all the more arresting because there is so much pathos implied in the way she variously clips, staggers, and extends each phrase; in the controlled huskiness of her voice, and in the lyrics themselves."

Speech and conversation added to the modern sensibility
of the record, which was also contemporary in its outlook.
On *Court and Spark*, Mitchell doesn't seem to be dreaming of
escape from the dilemmas of love as she did on *Blue* or *For the
Roses*. Her new attitude assumes a basic separation between the
sexes and resolves it into a resigned hopefulness that stops just
short of complacency. When in "Just Like This Train," Mitchell sings, "I used to count lovers like railroad cars / I counted
them on my side / lately I don't count on nothing / I just let
things slide," she is coming to terms with the negative aspects,
the possessiveness of romantic idealism. "The Same Situation,"
which has the narrator caught in a "struggle for higher achievements" and a "search for love / it don't seem to cease," was
recorded with strings, which surge forth with a lush and hopeful intensity. Most significantly, *Court and Spark* moved beyond
heartbreak; Mitchell doesn't sound quite so blue anymore,
even when she's breaking down. "Help Me" ("I think I'm falling in love again"), which is arguably Mitchell's most desperate
lyrical line, feels exhilarating with the buoyant backing of the
L.A. Express. The fresh, open sound of the track supports its
primary lyrical statement: "We love our lovin' / but not like
we love our freedom." The ode to serial monogamy captured
an increasingly mature attitude to romance in a culture seven
years beyond the guilt or rebellion of the Summer of Love. It
peaked at Number 7 in the first week of June 1974 and remains
Mitchell's only Top 10 song.

The album reached Number 2 on the *Billboard* chart and stayed on the chart for sixty-four weeks. *Court and Spark* wasn't the end of Mitchell's autobiographical songwriting, but it was the start of her long association with jazz, which found greater expression on her next two albums, *The Hissing of Summer Lawns* and *Hejira*, Mitchell's masterpiece. As much as she set the bar for transparency on *Blue*, Mitchell later helped propagate the idea that a singer is supposed to move on from autobiographical songwriting.

IN *COURT AND SPARK*'S TITLE TRACK the narrator seems to be recalling a time when someone tried to seduce her. The song has a detached rock sound rather than the intimacy of folk, but in the autobiographical tradition, this narrator closely resembles Mitchell herself. She identifies the seducer as a musician and places him in Berkeley with a reference to People's Park. At the song's end Mitchell sings that she, or the narrator, "couldn't let go of L.A., city of the fallen angels," implying that she decided to return home with the love affair unrequited or abandoned.

When Herbie Hancock hired me to write the press bio for his 2007 Grammy Award–winning *River: The Joni Letters* recording, which includes a cover of "Court and Spark," I spoke to Larry Klein, the record's producer. Klein is Mitchell's former husband of twelve years and musical collaborator of over two decades. Klein discussed his method of taking Hancock and his jazz musician colleagues through Mitchell's lyrics line by line, explicating their meaning as necessary. "Court and Spark" took some explaining, he said, because "hearing it for the first time—some of these guys were hearing these songs for the first time—you'd never grasp what the story is all about." He told the musicians the song was actually based on "a crazy fan approaching Joni and saying, 'This song was written for me, all your songs were written for me, right?' And her explaining, no, it wasn't. And he continues to make a case for the fact that it was and actually makes such a good case that she starts to actually feel like she understands what he's saying to a certain degree. So there's the idea of the narrator being in such a fragile position that they start believing what someone who's sitting on the edge of insanity is telling them." In the press bio I used Klein's quote on the origins of "Court and Spark" to elucidate its rather ominous reading by the jazz musicians—in their eerie reharmonization of the tune, they emphasize the danger of seduction and its sometimes menacing appeal to vulnerable people.

When Mitchell saw the press bio for Herbie's record, she was livid that the story was out, saying it was inaccurate. I believe her discomfort was based on her fear that the song would lose universality if its true impetus were known, that fans would stop hearing it as art and instead undertake an exercise in code cracking. There is some intrigue in decoding the lyrics in light of the song's background. "He thought for sure I'd seen him dancing up a river in the dark," refers to the crazy fan's mistaken assumption of himself as the narrator of her song "River" from *Blue*. In the second verse she sings, "He was playing on the sidewalk / For passing change," another faulty presumption by the fan, this time of the sidewalk musician character in her song "For Free"— then references his craziness in "burying the coins he'd made in People's Park."

But knowing about the episode that spurred the song only increases my admiration for Mitchell's artistry in transforming the personal into the universal. The song's power transcends a mere account of meeting some character with a "madman's soul" and "sleeping roll." Shifting for a verse into the voice of the crazy fan/potential lover, she sings, "You could complete me, and I'd complete you," which is the alluring fantasy of all prospective romances. "It seemed like he read my mind," she sings. "He saw me mistrusting him / And still acting kind." He can discern the narrator's true feelings behind her politeness; she yearns to be seen and understood. And like most of us, the narrator wants to be seduced: "The more he talked to me, you know, the more he reached me." But he doesn't reach her deeply enough, and she heads home to Los Angeles, where the incident lives on in her mind, as these things usually do for her.

The story behind the song humanizes Mitchell, a successful musician and insightful artist who shares the basic human traits of fragility and insecurity, who has a natural and even morbid interest in the reception of her music. Fortunately, the incident was striking enough that it stayed with Mitchell until she was compelled to spin it into a great song. As a story of failed seduction, "Court and Spark" is enduringly meaningful. The haunting nature of roads not taken is classic song material, as Norah Jones's phenomenally popular "Don't Know Why" also makes clear.

"I think the commonality is the key in that it's the reason why people appreciate something that's autobiographical," Larry Klein said. "If you take it down to the most essential part, the germ, it's 'Oh, you feel that? I feel that, too. I've been you in that situation.' And the way that that artist put it—the melody, and the way that person connected that melody to syllables, to a sequence of syllables, and to a sequence of sounds. The sound of that, and the meaning of it, evokes my experience that is in common with the person who wrote it." As the critic Robert Christgau has observed, Mitchell always wrote about what frightened not just her but also the "community." Even when her fears were personal, they were so fresh and well expressed that they resonated in hearts and minds beyond her. "Joni Mitchell's lyrics have always suggested emotional life with startling highs and lows and an attenuated middle," Christgau wrote in a review of *For the Roses*. "Just because she knows herself, she reveals how dangerous and attractive such a life can be, especially for women."

An artist seizes the passing moments that many of us forget, worries them through a whirl of sensitivity and sensibility, and elevates them into lasting artistic statements. If the song "Court and Spark" owes everything to the autobiographical impulse, it loses nothing to it.

6

The Breadth of Extremities

JONI MITCHELL'S *BLUE* ALBUM MOVES though scenes from the road like a musical diorama, but the primary color of its title comes from its sense of loss. Released in June 1971, it was in some ways a farewell to the 1960s, a private rumination on the passing of the decade's collective hopes, its innocence and ideals. *Blue* also accounts for a more personal loss: the end of Mitchell's romance with Graham Nash. Nash self-administered his own breakup therapy through his first solo album, *Songs for Beginners*—which was released just weeks before

Blue. In "Simple Man," a song he wrote for her, he clearly connected his music with their love's demise: "The ending of the tale is the singing of the song."

Another of Nash's songs for Mitchell, "Better Days," mourned the end of the life he had celebrated in his 1969 song "Our House." That earlier, happier song had established Joni and Graham's Lookout Mountain house in California as a very special place where "home" was an ongoing work of art made by love. Press articles elaborated on the myth, covering the couple's refined hippie pad with detailed enthusiasm worthy of *Architectural Digest*. "Antique pieces crowd tables, mantels, and shelves," gushed *Rolling Stone* in a 1969 article, and there were "castle-style doors and Tiffany stained glass windows; a grandfather clock and a Priestly piano." Unmarried shack-ups were still risqué enough that the writer perhaps felt he should aestheticize the couple. Graham, the article observed, was "perched on an English church chair," with Joni "in the kitchen, using the only electric lights on in the house," and "making the crust for a rhubarb pie."

In the bliss of infatuation, "Our House" came to Nash in only twenty minutes. "This thing happened between Joan and I where we went for breakfast at Art's Deli," Nash told me. "She saw a vase in a store that she really liked, and then we took the vase home and it was a gloomy day, and I said why don't I light a fire while you put the flowers in the vase you just bought? A completely ordinary experience. But I began to realize that every single person who'd ever had a relationship was going through a similar thing or had already been there." Joan was around to witness Graham's writing of "Our House," "because it happened so fast," he said. "By the time she got the flowers in the vase, the song was done."

Nash and Mitchell otherwise gave each other creative space. "I deliberately left when she was writing," he remembered. "I would support her until she disappeared into the Joni zone and then I would leave. Because if you're going to write about somebody and they're standing over your shoulder—that has to affect the way you write about whatever the situation is. So I would leave." As close as they were, they communicated to each other even more intimately through songs, and that conversation was "quite fascinating," said Nash: "And both incredibly sad and incredibly relief-giving." For him, there were revelations in their musical dialogues. In 1969, Mitchell wrote the song "Willy" for him, after his nickname, and in it the narrator says she would be Willy's lady all her life, but "he cannot hear the chapel's pealing silver bells." Nash said he was surprised "by the fact that she would have married me. I hoped, but I didn't know it. Because you know her grandmother was always kicking doors and wanting to live a different kind of life from being tied down by her grandfather and therefore she didn't express her own feelings and felt angry about that—that affected Joni a great deal. So when I found out that she would've married me if things had been a little better, it was quite shocking to me."

By the time "Willy" was released on *Ladies of the Canyon* in

April 1970, Mitchell was hippie vagabonding in Matala and having a fling with Cary Raditz (the "Carey" of her song title), on a break from her relationship with Nash after much discussion about ending it. One April morning, as Nash remembers it, he was at the Lookout Mountain house putting a new wood floor in the kitchen. He opened the door to a telegram from Joan. "The telegram said, 'If you hold sand too tightly, it runs through your fingers.' I knew it was over." In retrospect, Nash believes his insecurity about Mitchell's brilliance unraveled the relationship as much as her ambivalence toward commitment. "Joni and I loved each other deeply. But in many ways I never felt worthy. In certain ways toward the end I felt like I was holding her back."

Nash wrote "Simple Man," his please-take-me-back song, and premiered it alone in June 1970, without the virtuoso harmonies of band mates Crosby, Stills, and Young, whose vocals levitated even sad songs into hosannas. It was just Graham at the piano that evening at the Fillmore East, with Mitchell in the audience to hear doleful lines like, "Make me proud to be your man; only you can make me strong." That wasn't easy to do, he said: "It takes courage for you to lay your heart on the line for everyone to see and for everyone to knock around if they don't agree or don't like it."

Mitchell didn't go back to Graham, instead finding a quick rebound in a liaison with James Taylor in July 1970. James Taylor had opened for Mitchell in March 1969 at the Unicorn Coffee House in Boston, and they had spent some time talking at a songwriter's workshop at that summer's Newport Folk Festival. But the following summer at the Mariposa festival the timing was right, and throughout the fall and winter Mitchell and Taylor became the first couple of songwriting. The affair was as short and intense as Mitchell's fling with Leonard Cohen had been three years earlier. Nash claims now that it did not inspire any jealousy in him: "Why would you *not* want to hang out with James Taylor, for God's sake? Look at him." Still, the Joni-related songs on his *Songs for Beginners* album were shot through with pained confusion. In "I Used to Be a King," a response to Mitchell's "I Had a King," Nash rather defensively fantasized he was over her. Everything around him had "turned to rust"; though he dreamed all he'd have to do was sing, and he'd lift himself "way off the ground." Nash said Mitchell once told him she was surprised that he still missed her in bed, as he also mentioned in the song. Nash's statement, even only implied in song, is a rare violation of the code of gentlemanly restraint most of Mitchell's former lovers observe when discussing her.

Nash would go on to send Joni flowers for her birthday every year. "If two people were ever meant to be together, it was Graham and I," Mitchell told her friends, and she struggled with their breakup, putting her conflict and ambivalence into songs, too. But, to borrow from Blake, while Nash wrote songs of innocence, Mitchell wrote songs of experience. On *Blue*, she clearly confronted her deep feelings for him and chronicled her postromantic disillusionment. Certainly, she didn't fool herself into thinking no one was "gonna" break her heart again, as Nash sang on "I Used to Be a King." She detailed her conflict between love and freedom in self-realized torch songs; songs like "River" that bemoaned lost love but also took responsibility for losing it. As the critic Robert Hillburn has noted, at least in song, Mitchell is able to face her disappointments in love and deal with them in an instructive way. In "My Old Man," also about Nash, she especially struggled with her fundamental need to be an unbound creative spirit in a world that did not appreciate that quality in women. Her songs surpassed Nash's in their expression and evocation of feeling, and in their advanced use of metaphor, born of Mitchell's lyrical ability to elevate feelings into the universal sentiments of poetry.

One time a very close friend of Mitchell's asked her why she didn't write songs about him. "I'll never write about you," she said. "That's my way of putting people in the past, and I want to stay close to you." This friend claims that every song she wrote on the theme of romance was spurred by someone in particular, but he remains loyal to Mitchell in never identifying the guys behind the songs, because, he said, "It doesn't matter. The songs have more general meaning by the time they're recorded and certainly when they're heard." This transformation is partly why Mitchell eschews the term "confessional"; her songs take on so many functions and meanings that it is reductive to attribute them to any one person. "That entire album was for Joan," Nash also maintains, talking about *Blue*. "Was she talking about me occasionally? Yes. Was she talking about James occasionally? Yes. Was she talking about Leonard? Yes. Was she talking about America or Canada occasionally? Yes. But she made that album for herself."

And in making *Blue* her own, Mitchell layered broader themes into the subject of love. She conflated the fall of romance with the end of the 1960s' countercultural dreams. Earlier visions of fresh-dawned towns ("Morning Morgantown") and utopian cultures ("Woodstock") were gone, traded for existential pondering and for taking a hard look at herself. When she did invoke alternative lifestyles, as on the title track, it was to decry the nihilism into which the countercultural revolution had sunk: "Everybody's saying that hell's the hippest way to go, well, I don't think so. I'm going to take a look around it though." She listed some props of the revolution—"Acid, booze and ass / Needles, guns and grass"—then sang with sad irony that they only made for "lots of laughs."

"It's a description of the times," Mitchell affirmed. "There were so many sinking but I had to keep thinking I could make it through the waves. You watched that high of the hippie thing descend into drug depression. Right after Woodstock, then we went through a decade of basic apathy where my generation sucked its thumb and then just decided to be greedy and pornographic." In retrospect, everyone can see how the '60s went bad. But Mitchell's time frame for hindsight was always much tighter than most people's. What takes most of us a few years to realize seemed to take her only a few months. And though Mitchell had been right there in the 1960s, hanging and getting high with the hippie musician gods, as a Canadian she was enough of an outsider to gain the purchase necessary to serve as her generation's commentator on *Blue*.

The song "California" is in many ways *Blue*'s flagship. She wrote it "partially in Paris and partially in Ibiza" as her European adventure was wearing out and she was longing for America. Not the burned-out version of America she had fled, but a still fresh California, where she finished the song when she returned. In a way, it's a departure from the rest of *Blue*'s disillusionment with '60s ideals. Even though giving "peace a chance," she sings, "was just a dream some of us had," she wants to return to America and California, because they've become home to her. She'll "even kiss a Sunset pig," she sang, about her willingness to consort with the "enemy" on Sunset Boulevard. Mitchell likes to cite that lyric as an example of fans reading too much into her work, trying to imbue it with too much meaning. "I went into my pet store one day, where I've been going for years. The owner said to me: 'I've not wanted to ask, but I finally have to. My friends and I had heard sunset pig went back to a place in Malibu where they held up a pig to the sunset every night and someone had to be the one to kiss it. Is that right? What *is* a sunset pig?' I said, 'It's a cop on Sunset Boulevard.' 'Oh,' he said. I'm not trying to be cryptic but it seems like it is for some people."

The album, her first song-cycle—meaning each song is connected to the whole in terms of subject and sensibility— closes, significantly, on a plaintive note with "The Last Time

I Saw Richard." "It's not different than a Tennessee Williams play, that song," Mitchell told me. "It's got enough depth. You don't necessarily have to dig deeper—though every one of my songs works on a lot of levels. It works superficially, and if you want to dig in, there's some deep stuff to be found." Digging deeper into the song: it gave the era's end a date, 1968, when the narrator has a final meeting and argument with her friend in a Detroit café. He told her "all romantics meet the same fate someday," as she sings in tightly packed lines that twist and turn like jazz, "cynical and drunk and boring someone in some dark café." As the scholar Daniel Sonenberg has noted, her hopeful response in the face of this disenchantment worked, on another level, as a parable for the end of 1960s' idealism, which Mitchell chose to see as a transformative period: These "café days" were "only a dark cocoon before I get my gorgeous wings / And fly away."

Mitchell's weaving of "end of an era" themes among her romantic ones registered deeply with her fans at the time. In 1971, when *Blue* was released, they were feeling the losses of the 1960s. These themes may not be explicit to Mitchell's listeners of later generations, but they nevertheless enlarge the album's message of searching for wisdom in loss. Even someone like me, coming of age in the '90s, could grow up with *Blue*. When I first heard the record, I didn't know anything about the end of '60s counterculture—let alone Mitchell's troubled romance with Graham Nash—but was still eased into the end of innocence with her songs.

*   *   *

THE BEAT WRITERS of the 1950s set the stage for autobiographical songwriting, proposing the self and its journey as an acceptable literary topic. But unlike Bob Dylan and other songwriters who emerged in the '60s, Joni Mitchell claims the Beats had no creative impact on her. "I'm not a fan of the Beats," she told me. "I'm an Aquarian and long for a more graceful society. So the Beats to me, lying in their own puke and all . . . I was doing satire on the Beats in high school, but no one got it. It deserves recognition and like Dada will go down as a transitional thing. I'm not a fan of that pocket of art at all."

Mitchell's depiction of Beat literature is a caricature. She's probably not read much Gary Snyder, for example, whose elegant and often stark poetry on themes of nature and the self has little to do with hedonistic chaos. More significantly, she doesn't seem to value how much the Beats might have shown the way for her own self-revelation in songs. In making themselves their central characters, writers like Jack Kerouac demonstrated something critical. "You could write with your feelings as your compass," Rick Moody wrote of what he first learned from Kerouac's *On the Road*. "Accuracy about your human emotions was material enough." The Beats' antimaterialistic philosophy and soul-searching ethos seeped into the culture at large, and after influencing Dylan's turn to personal songwriting, positively saturated music scenes like Laurel Canyon in the late 1960s. The Beat practice of traveling to Europe to find yourself was still common a decade later in Mitchell's milieu, as was writing songs to capture the experience of the road.

Besides Kerouac's *On the Road*, Allen Ginsberg's 1956 *Howl* may have been the most influential work of Beat literature. In crowded lines so direct they incited an obscenity charge, he wrote an ode to his generation. Ginsberg looked back beyond modernist poets to Walt Whitman, who had employed an "I" as big as the cosmos as a means of immediacy and egalitarianism; Ginsberg looked back to William Blake for visionary ambition. He arrived at something very much his own, a confessional poem of desire. Ginsberg said what he achieved with *Howl* was "a breakthrough, not of universal consciousness or the social consciousness, but a discovery of my own consciousness, and then a proclamation of that. I'm trying to lay it out on the page: what is it I really desire." As critic M. L. Rosenthal wrote, Ginsberg "brought a terrible psychological reality to the surface with enough originality to blast American verse a hairsbreadth forward in the process." Rosenthal's diagnosis was borne out in Ginsberg's influence on poet Robert Lowell. After reading Ginsberg's work on an author tour in San Francisco in 1957, forty-year-old Lowell said his own work seemed "distant, symbol-ridden, and willfully difficult." Lowell was no convert to the Beats, and criticized their extravagant self-promotion. Still, after reading *Howl*, he wrote, his own "poems seemed like prehistoric monsters dragged down into the bog and death by their ponderous armor." And most important:

"I was reciting what I no longer felt." So Lowell went home and wrote in a new style, creating *Life Studies*, the poetry first labeled "confessional."

Bob Dylan read Ginsberg and had his own breakthrough in consciousness. When Dylan moved from his hometown of Hibbing, Minnesota, to Minneapolis in 1959, he said he "came out of the wilderness and just naturally fell in with the Beat scene, the Bohemian, Bebop crowd, it was all pretty connected." Dylan's high-octane literary regimen then "was Jack Kerouac, Ginsberg, Corso, and Ferlinghetti—*Gasoline, Coney Island of the Mind* . . . oh man, it was wild—*I saw the best minds of my generation destroyed by madness*—that said more to me than any of the stuff I'd been raised on. *On the Road*, Dean Moriarty, this made perfect sense to me." As Greil Marcus has suggested, Dylan's autobiographical "Like a Rolling Stone" probably owes more to Ginsberg's *Howl* than to any song.

Like Ginsberg, Jack Kerouac tried to get his immediate consciousness down on the page, with a combination of an improvisational jazz aesthetic and the Buddhist philosophy of "first thought best thought," a phrase Ginsberg often used. Capturing a first thought in the right words meant for Kerouac an exalted awareness of an image or emotion in all its nakedness. Gary Snyder had introduced Kerouac to Zen Buddhism, and Kerouac in turn introduced Ginsberg, who played at Zen until he met the Tibetan lama Chögyam Trungpa in 1971. Trungpa was a charismatic and controversial figure who is credited for helping popularize Buddhism in the West with his "Shambhala Training." Advocating a "crazy wisdom," or the "wisdom that's always been there," Trungpa capitalized on his Tibetan exoticism—he'd been raised on incarnation and enlightenment ceremonies involving a magical black crown—and used it to justify pretty much any behavior, including drinking and womanizing. Still, Trungpa's students, not least of all Ginsberg, insisted his was "a very rational and classical approach to Buddhism, in his real serious attention to sitting: 'Go sit, weeks and weeks and weeks, ten hours a day.'" Trungpa's basic approach was to begin with Shamatha meditation, a calming of the mind leading to sharpened awareness. Always seeking literary connections, Ginsberg said this meditative awareness was exemplified in William Carlos Williams's brief poems noting detail in the space around him: "I've had my dreams, like other men, but it has come to nothing. So that now I stand here feeling the weight of my coat on my shoulders, the weight of my body in my shoes, the breath pushing in and out at my nose—and resolve to dream no more."

After studying with Trungpa, Ginsberg improvised more poetry and song onstage, as he said, "trusting my own mind rather than a manuscript." Ginsberg liked to remember a time he read much of Kerouac's *Mexico City Blues* aloud to Trungpa, on a four-hour drive from Vermont to New York. Trungpa laughed all the way, Ginsberg said, and finally Ginsberg asked him what he thought of the poetry. Trungpa answered, "It's a perfect exposition of Mind."

*   *   *

JONI MITCHELL'S autobiographical songs of her Blue Period
are likewise expositions of mind, meditations on the complex
terrain of her feelings and thoughts. Mitchell's most perfectly
lucid exposition came on her 1976 album, *Hejira*, which means
a "flight from danger" in Arabic. Six years before, Mitchell
had traveled through Europe, fleeing her failed love affair with
Graham Nash and trying on hippie freedom for size. *Hejira*
was written after another breakup, this time with drummer
John Guerin, on a transcontinental trip in the spring of 1976
during the U.S. Bicentennial celebration. By then Mitchell was
in her early thirties and more ruminative than she had been
in 1970: after a few more rounds of relationships, finding and
losing love had come to matter less. But there was more than
just age and experience at work in *Hejira*. That year Mitchell
had a meeting with Ginsberg's guru, Chögyam Trungpa. This
audience with the lama proved very important to Mitchell,
giving her new perspective, helping her embrace the positive
and negative aspects of her character, its duality, without
judgment or striving for transcendence. This work toward self-
acceptance made *Hejira* the pinnacle of her autobiographical
songwriting.

In November 1975, Mitchell had joined up with Bob Dylan's Rolling Thunder Revue, which Dylan envisioned as a kind
of traveling gypsy circus and 1960s throwback. It involved cos-
tumed performances from Joan Baez, Roger McGuinn, T-Bone

Burnett, Ronee Blakley, and whoever else washed up and could hang on the tour. From the beginning, Joni was ambivalent about being part of what she called Rolling Thunder's "narcissistic mess."

"I went to see a show, and it was intriguing because a bunch of Indians showed up. But Bob and Joan [Baez] are very competitive. To subordinate myself to them on that tour was the worst career move I could have made. Management was calling and saying, 'Come home, what are you doing, what are you doing?' But I had a mystical experience while I was out there that was personal and coincidental and so I stayed."

Playwright and actor Sam Shepard was also on board to write an on-the-spot-film script for the musical magic bus tour. In an impressionistic journal, which he later published as the *Rolling Thunder Logbook*, Shepard chronicled the tour's big personalities and their decadence—"A hundred bucks' worth of Valiums are delivered to the Niagara Hilton like so much Chicken Delight"—and how the pressure of trying to film it all wore on him: "More talk of shooting concerts. More talk on how to organize scenes. How to get Dylan into the picture. Sara [Dylan's wife]. Joni Mitchell. Baez. It's almost that the sheer overkill of available talent is busting us wide open."

Besides pills, the Rolling Thunder pharmacopoeia included

vast amounts of cocaine. As Mitchell has remembered, "They asked me how I wanted to be paid, and [it was like] I ran away to join the circus: Clowns used to get paid in wine—pay me in cocaine because everybody was strung out on cocaine." Cocaine addled her and gave her insomnia but also stimulated her songwriting. On tour, she wrote a song called "Dreamland," which she gave to Roger McGuinn, formerly of the Byrds, when he asked her for one. McGuinn wrote about the episode in his ongoing blog memoir (which he somewhat confusingly writes in the third person):

Joni Mitchell was habitually writing lyrics in her black and white composition book while the tour bus "Phydeaux" rolled down the highway. One of the songs in that notebook was "Dreamland." When Roger asked her for a song to record on his album, she gave it to him but wasn't quite sure if one line would work for Roger. She smiled when Roger suggested the "folk tradition" of changing lyrics to match the gender of the singer. He would change "Dorothy Lamour sarong" to "an Errol Flynn sarong." There were so many words in the song, he wondered if anyone would notice the difference or even laugh at the image of Errol Flynn in a sarong.

McGuinn recorded the song for his 1976 album *Cardiff Rose*. Joni didn't record "Dreamland" until 1977 on *Don Juan's Reckless Daughter*. It takes off on a happy 1974 trip to Brazil

with John Guerin and turns it into a tongue-in-cheek adver-
tisement for exotic escapism. Propelled by Airto Moreira's
Brazilian drumming, "Dreamland" was identified by Stephen
Holden as "Mitchell's greatest third-person song: a frighten-
ing, funny parody of how television and advertising corrupt
ideas by turning them into commercial products with a putative erotic value." While she worked on new songs during Rolling Thunder, Mitchell performed "Edith and the Kingpin" and
"Don't Interrupt the Sorrow" from her 1975 album *The Hissing
of Summer Lawns*. Like "Dreamland," these were third-person
songs, the character sketches and social commentary she'd
lately been favoring over her earlier autobiographical material. Mitchell's fans weren't happy about the change. "Don't
Interrupt the Sorrow" is about people in a bar, but in some
respects, Joni has said, her fans directed the sentiment back to
her literally. "If some people had their way, they'd just want
me to weep and suffer for them for the rest of my life, because
people live vicariously through their artists. And I had that
grand theme for a long time: Where is my mate? Where is my
mate? Where is my mate? I got rid of that one."

She wasn't quite rid of it, though. Among the strong egos
and intense social scene of Rolling Thunder, Mitchell again
turned inward. "I studied ego, that's all I did on Rolling Thunder. I watched these malformed egos as they interacted with
my own and ended up delving into my own malformed ego."
That self-scrutiny led Mitchell back to autobiography. At the
Revue's November 26 concert in Augusta, Maine, Mitchell in-

troduced a new song called "Coyote," saying it had been written the previous day. "Coyote" was the first single off *Hejira* and was based on her passing affair with Sam Shepard during the tour. Throughout her Blue Period, Mitchell was inspired by the emotional intensity of love and sex, renewed in relationship after relationship, which gave her the lyrical momentum she needed for writing. "Coyote" was Mitchell's most flippant song about love. "No regrets," she sang—the affair was not going anywhere, anyway: "I'm up all night in the studios and you're up early on your ranch." (For his part, while on tour Shepard fantasized about scrapping the Rolling Thunder film project and resuming his cowboy role: "Just wanna go back home," he wrote in his journal. "Be in the mountains. Near horses. Near my woman." His woman at home, that is.) Like the other Rolling Thunder players, Mitchell wrote, she and Coyote were just muddling through, taking their "temporary lovers and their pills and powders to get them thru this passion play." The difference between Shepard's and Mitchell's experiences in the Rolling Thunder Revue was that Shepard seemed to know what he wanted on the tour and what rubbed him the wrong way; Mitchell was, as always, porous and open, assimilating into the tour for better or worse in ways she'd have to work out later. "Talk about a ship of fools," Joni said. "Everybody was certifiable on that tour. They were drinking and taking drugs to the max. It was really maxed-out insanity. I could only take so much before I needed to dry out myself."

In January 1976, Mitchell left the Neverland on wheels

that was Rolling Thunder and set out with her own band to tour *The Hissing of Summer Lawns*. In early February, the tour made a stop in Memphis, where she had a meeting with blues musician Furry Lewis that was the basis for "Furry Sings the Blues." At the end of the month, Mitchell canceled the rest of the tour—perhaps because of problems with John Guerin, with whom she was breaking up; perhaps because of poor reception from fans to the *Hissing* album; perhaps because of coke-addled post–Rolling Thunder existential angst; or most likely because of some combination of all three. Back home in Los Angeles in March, Mitchell was convinced by a couple of friends—an old boyfriend from Australia and a young flight steward who still lived with his parents—to join them on a cross-country trip to Damariscotta, Maine, on a desperately gallant mission to recover the ex-boyfriend's daughter from his mother-in-law's home. "We were going to kidnap his daughter from the wicked twin grandmothers," Mitchell said. "The mother was in a mental institution." She and the two men drove east across the northern United States. When their car broke down, Mitchell bought a secondhand Mercedes, which also kept breaking down. Not far into the trip, her L.A. Express guitarist Robben Ford invited her to Boulder for the previously mentioned audience with Chögyam Trungpa, and she decided to meet him. It wasn't such an outlandish or impulsive visit for Joni. She'd been interested in Eastern spirituality ever since Leonard Cohen gave her the *I Ching* in 1967. The *I Ching* had led her to the Medicine Wheel, which regularly inspired and informed her creative work. Besides, she'd heard Allen Ginsberg mention Trungpa on the Rolling Thunder tour. She was curious.

MITCHELL HAS TOLD ME the story of her initial meeting with Trungpa on a couple of occasions, first in a 2004 phone interview and again in the summer of 2008 during dinner with friends near her second home in British Columbia. At such dinners, Mitchell is accustomed to playing a kind of hip queen holding court for her awed subjects. Even at sixty-five Mitchell has an undeniable glamour—that night in BC she wore loose white linens and a tan cap, exuding a cool regality. If people aren't impressed by her presence, they certainly are when she begins sharing big ideas and telling tour de force road stories in her liltingly musical Canadian cadences. Mitchell's speech unfolds in paragraphs, rich in insight and metaphor. It's no exaggeration to say she's usually striving for truth or beauty as she talks.

That night I was the only one besides Mitchell who was saying much. Seated next to me was a friend of hers who works as a kind of Reiki healer. I asked this woman if she tried to be funny when conducting her healings, since, I said lightly, "Humor can be a sign of enlightenment—it might make your clients trust you." Mitchell laid into me. "Humor is no sign of enlightenment," she said, raising her voice. "Humor is necessary, but it's not a sign of anything. Don't put it that way, because it's ignorant." Everyone at the table froze over their salads. The Great Goddess's ire had been raised. But I wasn't going to be cowed—for all the deference Mitchell expects, beneath it she craves discussion, or "riffing," as she puts it, in musician parlance.

(The next evening, I should mention, Mitchell apologized for "going after" me. With amused self-disclosure, she said, "I get kind of agitated, I'm finally going in for a 'treatment,' so that I won't be so rrrr-rrrr-rrr, so terrier-like." She looked down at Coco, her Jack Russell terrier.

"At least I know where you stand," I said.

She answered, "Oh, you *never* have to worry about that with me.")

So when Mitchell called my comment ignorant, I asked, "Well, what about Trungpa? Didn't he say you needed 'heart and *humor* and humility,' as you wrote in a song?" Her eyes lit up, and she put down her fork. When Mitchell's in an argument and the stakes are raised, she's even more invested in spinning a good yarn. "Now, Trungpa, he was about something altogether different," she said, launching into an enhanced story of their meeting.

"I was drug to see Trungpa by an aggressive woman, a musician's wife. I know it's better to follow Miles Davis's rule of having no old ladies on the road, but she insisted on coming. One time backstage in the green room, I was about to leave the room when she yells out, 'Who did this?' Someone had spilled some almonds. On the road, she wouldn't ride the bus. She had to be in the car with me. One time I got in the car and she says, 'You can't smoke in here.' I said, 'You can't ride in here.' So that was all just to clarify the kind of pain in the ass this girl was."

So it was this "pain in the ass" woman—Robben Ford's wife—who actually took Mitchell to see Trungpa.

"Everything I felt about her, I transferred all her qualities to Trungpa, so I went in with attitude, looking down on him. Trungpa asked me what my problem was, and my problem seemed really big. I was in a triangle with these two guys who were traveling with me—the one who was an old lover from a long time ago, and there was a mild flirtation with the other, the youthful spirit. I can't get out of it, I told him. I'm in between these guys. Well, I could get out, but it was my car we were driving to Maine. So I tell him my problem and he goes, 'How lovely.' In that British accent, and in a tone so mischievous and so facetious that there was no condescension. I've had friends who loved me and when I told them problems they sympathized, but this was the only time someone realized my problems with no condescension. It wasn't anything I'd ever encountered. So it completely disarmed me and I lost all my attitude. I'm looking at him and I realized I was in the presence of the greatest psychologist I'd ever seen. So then, I looked up to him. I flattered him. I tried to win his affection. But I busted myself. I said, 'I'm flattering you.' I said it right out loud."

Though it was progress for Mitchell to cease her anxious roundelay of superiority and inferiority, Trungpa wasn't satisfied. He said she should just quit analyzing: First thought best thought. Mitchell argued that was impossible for her; as an artist she had to analyze (this perceived conflict between art and spirituality still plagues her today). When Trungpa next asked her, "Well, do you believe in God?" Mitchell reverted to her condescending pose.

"I said, 'Yes,' and then—this was such an asshole comment—I produce this bag of coke and say, 'This is my God and this is my prayer.' He didn't flinch, but his nose started to flare. And I thought, *Does he want some [coke]?* [*Laughing*]. That's when he started breathing, and there was a big hole on that one because I didn't notice I was being zapped. And then I had no sense of 'I' or me, no self-consciousness for three days."

There is some precedent for this magical occurrence: in Tibetan Buddhism, there is a phenomenon called *rigpa tsel wang*, which is a state of enlightenment directly transmitted from teacher to student. I'd heard this story before, and Mitchell's loss of self for three days following her meeting with

Trungpa had always sounded really good to me, if a little far-fetched. That night at dinner I told Joni about my own meeting with Trungpa's son, Sakyong Mipham, for a 2006 National Public Radio interview. The Sakyong assumed the leadership of Trungpa's Shambhala lineage in 1995, a few years after his father's death. I went jogging with the Sakyong, a marathoner who credits meditation for his running success.

At the end of that interview, I had somewhat facetiously asked the Sakyong if he could do to me what his father had done to Mitchell—remove my sense of "I" for three days.

"What if you turn off the tape and we do it together?" the Sakyong had answered with raised eyebrows, and I had the impression this gesture was a suggestive allusion to the rumor that Mitchell and Trungpa had slept together. I was silent. The Sakyong recovered his holy man composure and said, "What if the 'I' was never there?" He stood up and left the room—and left me to ponder the question.

After I told Joni this story, she said the Sakyong responded as such because he doesn't have powers and is "living in the shadow of his father, in bewilderment." That may be true. The Sakyong certainly doesn't have his father's crazy-wisdom magnetism or his lifestyle. I believe the Sakyong's response may also reflect a fundamental growth in Western Buddhist practice. Back in the '70s, Trungpa used the occasional spiritual trick to reel in practitioners, and rock stars like Mitchell, who traded in charisma, often needed a taste of the supernatural to penetrate their egos. In the intervening decades, Western

Buddhism has become more pragmatic, and the Shambhala training now presents losing the ego and awakening the mind as processes brought about by the long, hard work of meditation practice.

I asked Mitchell what happened in those three days of no self. What if she went into a restaurant to order food with no "I"? After her audience with Trungpa in Boulder, Mitchell said, she and her two companions headed northeast toward Maine, stopping over in Toronto.

"We went into a restaurant in Toronto, me and these two guys. We went to a restaurant, and while we were in there, the object of my flirtation—a very young spirit who had some psychological depth but was very childlike—he stood up on a chair in this restaurant in Toronto, and was just being silly. All around in the restaurant everyone was glaring. In that state, after meeting Trungpa, I had no sense of self and other. Normally I would be separating myself from his conduct, you know. But in this state, I didn't; at the same time I felt the total disapproval of the room. So I said to the room, 'He's acting like a real jerk, isn't he?' But I said it in a purely factual way, like Trungpa had said 'How lovely' to me. With no condescension. So I say, 'He's acting like a jerk,' and the room, every face lights up and relaxes. The guy on the chair looks down at me and he goes *what*, trying to feel insulted. He's very psychological, his eyes are searching ding, ding, ding, ding, ding, my face, but there's no 'I' thing there. He was trying to find the thing that's condescending. It's not there."

It seems to me this man very well may have felt condescended to after being chastised in public. And Mitchell said she lost her blissful state of selflessness three days after meeting Trungpa, when she had her first "I" thought, which was "I am enlightened." But the effects of her meeting with Trungpa lingered: "What I took away from this is that two people cannot be looking up or down at each other. In order for Trungpa to reach me and put me in a state of grace, we had to be on the level. Once I stopped condescending or flattering, once it leveled out, we had a really good rapport."

MITCHELL'S VISIT with Trungpa had creative consequences, too, in the meditative songs of *Hejira*.

"Everything about the journey was unusual. But the journey back was reflective. I went and bought all Trungpa's books to understand this abnormal consciousness that had occurred and how he'd done it to me. And the journey back was one of detoxing basically from Rolling Thunder the year before . . . [a] process of cleaning up from the drug habit. So that whole album was written coming out of the fog and having been really delivered from the fog into a state of absolute mental health temporarily with no

'I' thing. The journey was quite an exceptional journey, mentally and physically, and I think that the writing on that album reflected it."

As she traveled on with her friends and then by herself, Mitchell tried to *write* her way back to that temporary state of equanimity, to *compose* herself into the grace of those three days. This gave her an evolved outlook on the long-standing focus of her work, which her husband Larry Klein once called "an inquiry into the nature of modern love." The six songs she wrote after parting with her companions all have the dreamlike intensity of her solitary cross-country driving that spring, and reflect her philosophical shift after meeting with Trungpa.

As they arrived in New England, Mitchell had a brief affair with the object of her flirtation, he of the immature restaurant antics, which she said is "partly chronicled" on *Hejira*'s "A Strange Boy." Trungpa's philosophy shows up explicitly in the song when Mitchell explains that the strange boy's "crazy wisdom" was "holding on to something wild." Another of Trungpa's early teachings explored "Alcohol as Poison and Medicine" (an interesting topic, since Trungpa was a heavy drinker). In this song, she and her lover get drunk "on alcohol, and on love, the strongest poison and medicine of all." A more pervasive if subtle sign of Trungpa's influence is evident on *Hejira* in the new distance she has from her desires. At the beginning of her Blue Period, Mitchell's songs wrestled with the idea of romance: the need to "renew" someone in "All I Want";

the conflict between self and other, between egoless love and lonely freedom in "My Old Man." In "A Strange Boy," she realizes the fruitlessness of trying to remedy a lover's faults, or hers, the futility of trying to make an affair into something it's not. To paraphrase her lyrics: This strange boy asked her to be patient, and she failed, crying, "Grow up!" As the smoke cleared, he said, "Give me one good reason why!" With her more detached perspective on love, the narrator's feeling for the strange boy "comes and goes" more naturally, "like the pull of moon on tides." One moment she is "surf rising," the next she's "parched ribs of sand at his side." "All I Want" ended with a desire to make a lover feel free. This song ends without any longing for what could be or might have been. There is only a simple description of the lovers' passion in a New England hotel as "fire in the stiff-blue-haired-house-rules."

But if Mitchell's wandering narrator in *Hejira* was more coolly distant than before, she still took on her epic conflict between love and freedom. After parting with the two men, Joni stayed for a time in New York, where one day she and photographer Joel Bernstein took the Staten Island ferry to the Mandolin Brothers shop. That trip launched "Song for Sharon," Mitchell's open letter to a childhood friend, which she wrote that evening on cocaine. Sharon ended up with a "husband and a family and a farm," the life Mitchell imagined she'd have. Mitchell ended up with a string of broken romances, with what she sang was love as a "repetitious danger"—but she'd learned to "accept the changes, at least better than I used to do." As she travels in the song, Mitchell contrasts the geography of her memory with the present landscape, placing herself in the setting of New York's Bleecker Street while remembering back to Maidstone, where she and Sharon had gone to weddings and love had stimulated Mitchell's girlish illusions.

Mitchell had originally named her title track the rather unmemorable "Traveling." "I was looking for a word that meant 'running away with honor,' leaving the dream with honor," Mitchell told me. "There isn't any word for it in the English language. And 'hejira,' I found it by just reading the dictionary. It stuck out on the page because of the shape of it. With the 'j' it was an unusual-looking word. Leaving always has a cowardly connotation except for 'exodus,' which is associated with Israel. Hejira was Mohamed leaving Mecca. So it is only those two traditions, which have at least in part of their culture an interest in wisdom—not many cultures do—that had a word which meant there can be a time to leave that isn't just going AWOL."

The song is also a step up from standard songwriting. Composed on the road with only a guitar, *Hejira*'s songs are sparser than the ambitious horn-rich tracks of her previous two albums, *Court and Spark* and *Hissing of Summer Lawns*. Her harmonies, however, are anything but standard. The instrumental introduction and bridges of "Hejira" are in a different key than the lyrical passages, creating a sense of languid movement from one figurative place to another. These picturesque musical bridges suggest the shifting landscapes of her journey.

Into this open, panoramic sound enter the restlessly fluid bass lines of Jaco Pastorius, whose first contribution to Mitchell's music was on this track. Pastorius was a jazz musician who was then working with Weather Report. "Most bassists go plodding along at the bottom," Mitchell told me. "But Jaco was the bass player of my dreams. He was completely unruly; you couldn't handle him at all. He was like a wild man." Pastorius ignored bar lines and the traditionally supportive role of the bass. And he could draw pictures with music. His first few, soaring lines in "Hejira" manage to quote Stravinsky and evoke the character of Mitchell's questing narrator.

Mitchell calls Jaco her "kindred spirit," and that's evident when his bass parries and thrusts with her vocals in duets that reflect her lyrical theme of duality. Mitchell has said "Hejira" explores her reasons for running away from Guerin—here she sings that she is a "defector from the petty wars that shell-shock love away." "Song for Sharon" implies that she and Sharon envied each other's lives; in "Hejira" she revisits the issue, suggesting that neither life offers an ideal solution: "it never has been easy whether you do or you do not resign, whether you travel the breadth of extremities or stick to some straighter line." Mitchell had charted her romantic blues from the beginning of her recording career: "I Had a King," from her first album, was about her failed marriage. In "Both Sides, Now," she'd embraced melancholy and equanimity, singing of the end of her naïveté: "something's lost, but something's gained." But she'd always regretted the loss of ideals, of commitment. In

"Hejira," she found solace in being neither here nor there: she found "comfort in melancholy," as "natural as the weather in this moody sky today."

Guerin was still on Mitchell's mind when she stayed in Savannah at the DeSoto Hilton on Tybee Island, "an old, funky lighthouse-keeping place on the beach," as she has remembered it. There she gained a little distance on her reflections, enough to write a lighthearted torch song called "Blue Motel Room." Many blues songs carry a double-consciousness and are performed with buoyancy in their self-pity—a bounce of confidence that everyone has felt the same things. In "Blue Motel Room" Mitchell sings, "I got the blues inside and outside my head," taking a break from the hard work of expressing feelings with her typical sophistication and seriousness. If Guerin will only "lay down" his "sneaking round the town," she promises she'll "lay down the highway." She plays at the catharsis of the blues, as if singing a few simple lines will get the difficulties with him out of her system. Mitchell also remembers stocking her room at the DeSoto with health food and vitamins and running on the beach in the mornings to clean the drugs from her body and "recover from the physical and mental abuse of Rolling Thunder."

Sporting a red wig and renaming herself "Charlene Latimer," Mitchell went down to Florida and headed back west along the Gulf of Mexico. "My driver's license had expired. Without it, I had to get my car back to the West Coast. I had to follow truckers and drive only in daylight hours. The truckers kind of cocoon you when there's cops ahead." Mitchell told the writer Doug Fisher that down South, where hard rock and country music dominated the airwaves, Mitchell was unknown. "It was a relief," she has said. "I was able, like *The Prince and the Pauper*, to escape my fame under a false name and fall in with people and enjoy ordinary civilian status." But Mitchell wasn't always as anonymous as she would have liked to be. When she checked into the Grand Hotel in Point Clear, Alabama, she tried to pass herself off as "Joan Black." "Sure, Ms. Mitchell, whatever you say," the hotel barman said. In Alabama she met DiGi and Jet Broughton, two local musicians, and told them about hanging out with some beach bums down in Gulf Shores—until they figured out who she really was. Mitchell went into a Winn-Dixie grocery store to get cold cuts for those friends and heard a Muzak version of "Both Sides, Now." After that, she told the Broughtons, the song would always make her think of bologna.

Heading west into the "burning desert" of Arizona, Mitchell wrote "Amelia" for Amelia Earhart, the famous and ill-fated aviatrix who died—disappeared—into the ocean midflight. Mitchell's poeticism gains complexity in the song as she juxtaposes images to build meaning. In Ezra Pound's theory of the "ideogram," which is his take on the machinery of metaphor, two contrasting images don't create a third image; they create an idea. In "Amelia," Mitchell sings that she sees "six jet planes" and calls their vapor trails the "hexagram of the heavens" and then likens them to the "the strings of [her] guitar." These serial metaphors project the idea of Joni and Amelia merging in a surreal flight. "Well, I saw six white lines in the sky," Mitchell told me. "And then it was just my own private mental association. The first thing I think is 'Ah, it looks like six guitar strings' then also the first change in the *I Ching* is six straight lines, and it's the symbol for the creative—the hexagram of the heavens. The first change in the *Chinese Book of Changes* is two trigrams of three straight lines, one over the other—each one symbolizing the heavens, so it's the heavens over the heavens. And together they form the creator. So that's what that means."

As on "Hejira," the song's music moves back and forth between two keys without ever settling into one. In critic Tom Manoff's astute analysis, this makes for a hypnotic, "floating" background that, like Amelia and Joni, never reaches home.

> The effect of this harmonic design, coupled with the slow, gently swaying rhythms, seems to "open up into the sky." Superimposed upon the basic structure are whining, "cool," electric sounds, often dissonant, that haunt the musical background. The musical elements support a carefully balanced poetical structure. In each verse of six lines, the harmonic and rhythmic tension reach a maximum level in the third line, which causes the following three lines to come gently tumbling out in perfect acoustic symmetry.

The song's only resolution comes in its refrain: "Amelia, it was just a false alarm." For Earhart, the false alarm was the possibility of rescue; for Mitchell, it was the possibility of a romantic solution to her existential angst. Here Mitchell was at her most revealing: "Maybe I've never really loved / I guess that is the truth / I've spent my whole life in clouds at icy altitudes."

The final song in *Hejira*'s tightly interwoven cycle is "Refuge of the Roads," which is a commentary on her entire journey. The song—one of the few Mitchell admits is *about* anyone in particular—is about Trungpa, whom in her lyrics she calls a "friend of spirit, he drank and womanized." After she left him, she sings, she had good times on the road when she lived in the moment. Then she started analyzing again—against Trungpa's advice—and a "thunderhead of judgement" was once again "gathering in my gaze." She hopes this thunderhead can become the clouds of Michelangelo, "muscular with gods and sungold," shining on her, the witness, in the "refuge of the roads." "After enlightenment or nirvana or Buddha mind or whatever you want to call it, having experienced that, I went back to normal," Mitchell explained years later. "It was back to the critical capacity of an artist from this awakened state I'd been in. That's kind of described in 'Refuge of the Roads': 'But then I started analyzing.' And it did make most people nervous [*laughs*]. They didn't want to know what I was seeing."

Mitchell's constant search for big visions in small things pays off most richly in this song. She ends it and the album with a telling image, the famous photograph of the earth, replicated on a calendar hanging in a roadside gas station. The same image would later illuminate the backdrop for her ballet

The Fiddle and the Drum: "There's a circle hanging over the stage and NASA photographs of Earth from outer space—that same image keeps coming up by daylight and by night, which is a scary sight to see that much electricity, you know, to see the planet has a fever. But on the trip that worked itself into *Hejira*, I felt as if I was constantly in outer space looking back." From the photo's perspective, she sings in "Refuge of the Roads," you couldn't see a city, forest, highway, or "me here least of all." After months on the road, Mitchell—or her narrative persona, at least—has found a way to both experience *and* describe the absence of self she'd had in those three blissful days after she met Trungpa.

Mitchell suffered no crisis of self-exposure after recording *Hejira* as she had with *Blue*, although *Hejira* was no less honest and hyper-expressive an album. Her lyrics acknowledged that she was as unsettled in love in her mid-thirties as she'd been six years before. Like *Blue*, *Hejira* resounded with accessible emotion: each note on the album reflects and illuminates her lyrics; most songs are written in the first person, so listeners can identify with her persona to the point of assuming it. "You know I think really what it documented?" Mitchell said. "I think it gave melancholy its proper due—the melancholy of mate bonding difficulty. And I think that's why it affected the gay male population as deeply as it did. It picked up a big gay following." But there is a qualitative difference in the self-observation she records on *Hejira*. In many ways, the album was Mitchell's own response to the question she'd asked on *Blue*'s

"California": "Will you take me as I am?" She'd learned how to take herself as she was. And in examining her own character with discrimination and empathy, Mitchell absolved herself of the need to write autobiographical songs. In reconciling with her own indecisiveness, Joni put an end to her Blue Period. With self-acceptance, Mitchell could move beyond autobiographical songwriting.

She would of course go on writing personal songs. "Don Juan's Reckless Daughter," the title track of her next album, was even written at the same time as *Hejira*'s "Coyote" and she often performed the two songs as a suite. And on 1982's *Wild Things Run Fast*, Mitchell wrote the only lyric she admitted might fall into the confessional category, besides "I'm selfish and I'm sad" from "River." In "Man to Man" she sings: "I don't like to lie, but I sure can be phony when I get scared. I stick my nose up in the air—stoney, stoney Joni when I get scared."

> "When I sang that the first night in a concert in Berkeley, the whole audience gasped. They gasped! A huge sound of everybody sucking in their breaths. Now obviously I didn't intend it to be shocking, but obviously it was. So when you get an audience gasping like that, you've hit a human truth. Everybody in that audience knew that they get phony when they get scared. But they didn't want me to say it."

On *Don Juan's Reckless Daughter* and beyond, however, she would be more interested in musical experimentation than personal revelation, and turn to social commentary and story-telling as her primary lyrical pursuits. That outward focus produced some of her most inspired work. Albums like *Mingus* and projects like her ballet have just as much philosophical luster and emotional energy as her earlier personal songwriting.

Still, I believe Joni Mitchell is at heart an autobiographical artist. Here are a few final words from her.

"When I write my memoirs, I'm not going to write very much about all the songs, the music business. That's like a dream. Basically, there's kind of a mystical thread that runs through my life, and I could write a really interesting book just about how mysterious life is. I'm kind of test-ing the stories. I keep telling my tales to everyone—I wax very autobiographical to anyone who will listen and even those who won't."

Stuff Joni Likes or Even Loves

JONI MITCHELL FREQUENTLY COMES OFF IN published interviews as bitter about the state of modern culture and disparaging of other songwriters and much else. I've heard some of that myself. She told me most of the material written about her is "good for insomnia." People who call her "confessional" have IQs "lower than room temperature." Don't get her started on Jackson Browne, the Catholic Church, or modern medicine.

I always thought this negative portrayal in print was a shame, because it's not fully reflective of Joni's intelligence and lust for life. Also, I prefer to hear about what artists like without the editing of interviewers, so that I can make my own conclusions about how the themes or books or songs or places they admire might play into their work.

I've heard firsthand a number of things Joni likes. Most of this list comes from my own interviews, though I've drawn from other sources if she spoke about something more expansively elsewhere. And often the praise for one thing comes with a dig at another. She just can't seem to stop discerning.

PINBALL

"Isn't it great how sometimes you can feel like you're part of the machine?"

HER BALLET

"It's my favorite thing I ever did. The ballet. It's my favorite project. The most joyous project."

CIGARETTES

"It's a focusing drug. Everybody should just be forced to smoke."

SOME SHORT-STORY WRITERS

"You heard of Alice Munro? Boy! I connect with her. She's a fellow Canadian and she writes about things I lived through. But I kinda slept through them. I didn't absorb them like her—detailed memories of childhood, family gatherings, events. I used to look to Dylan or Neil [Young] for songwriting inspiration but now, there's no one really cutting it, so you gotta turn to the short story tellers—Munro, Raymond Carver, the dirty realists. Since *The Hissing of Summer Lawns*, I've been a frustrated short story writer but whereas Carver makes me think I can write short stories, Munro makes me think I can't." ("Idol Talk," Sean O'Hagan, *New Musical Express*, June 4, 1988)

SOME FILMMAKERS

"Tarkovsky—it's hard on the tailbone but it lingers in your mind, stays with you. That's why I did this video with Anton [Corbijn, director of *My Secret Place*], I knew he was a big Tarkovsky fan when I saw the Depeche Mode video and those close-ups of wind and grass. Beautiful. I like Fellini too. I thought he was a surrealist until I went to Italy. Now I realise he's a graphic realist!" ("Idol Talk," Sean O'Hagan, *New Musical Express*, June 4, 1988)

BEING A POOL SHARK

"We were just up in Banff and there was a pool hall there, and I went in and pretty soon I had a rep as a shark. And this made everybody nervous. I had a game with a guy who was really a pretty good player. I had a good route and I had the four ball and then I was on the eight ball and I had a really easy shot. It was direct into the pocket and all the guys came and hovered around . . it was such an easy shot. And I didn't put bottom on the ball and it followed it in.

It was perfect. So I laughed. And the guy was . . . it was kind of a role reversal. They thought that I threw the game intentionally, so he couldn't enjoy the victory. But I screwed up. It was perfect."

HER PLACE IN BRITISH COLUMBIA

"Every day there's something memorable. I step out on my deck in good weather or bad and I just . . . my soul is a big hallelujah. But here I live so simply and small and I'm the gardener and the cook and I have chores and every time I step outside, I say, 'I can't believe I'm living here.' I'm just so grateful."

SOME DYLAN

" 'Positively 4th Street' was inspirational to me, and after that, 'Idiot Wind' and 'Tangled Up in Blue.' "

JAZZ TRUMPETER AMBROSE AKINMUSIRE

"There were three trumpet players at Herbie Hancock's tribute for the Monk Institute [2007]. I was in the back and I heard the first one and nothing was happening, I heard the second one, nothing happening, we talked all the way through it. When the third one came on, I shushed everyone up in the room and I listened to this guy. He was so fresh. His tone, everything was like a total original, which is hard on any instrument at this point to have an identity. So I'm out in the wings afterwards and this kid came up to me. His head was bigger than his body like he'd had poor nutrition as a child or something. He introduced himself and I said, 'Are you in one of the bands?' and he said, 'No I'm one of the trumpet players,' and I said, 'Oh, which one are you?' and he went 'The third one,' and I went, 'Oh my God,' and it's so hard for me to pay an effusive compliment, it's almost embarrassing to me, and I went 'Aahhh, you are a killer! Your tone is so original, your choice of notes . . .' So I went, 'Where do you dribble off of? You're not like Dizzy and you're not like Miles, you're so . . .' And do you know what he said? He said, 'You . . . you.' "

NIETZSCHE

"Nietzsche speaks about poets: 'A poet is the vainest of the vain. He is the peacock of peacocks. Before the ugliest of water buffalo he fans his tail. He muddies his waters so that he might appear deep.' In *Thus Spake Zarathustra*, he said, 'How can you speak so negatively about the poets? Is Zarathustra not also a poet?' Of course he is, how else can he know? But I see a new poet on the horizon, he is a penitent of spirit. And he writes in his own blood."

MEDICINE WHEEL

"The idea of the medicine wheel is one I've lived with for many years. It's an idea that has as its rudiments a belief that the four directions influence our perspectives. The north influences intellect. The south influences emotionality. The east, the rising sun, influences clarity. And the west influences sensitivity and tactile intelligence, and the look-within place, the deepening place. If you believe in this, then living with it on a daily basis and making observations, it teaches you. One of its functions is the attempt to speak a whole truth and in that function, it's referred to as the Chief's Wheel. This means that if you get up to speak in front of a group of people, you understand that they are perceiving you and perceiving what you're saying from one of the eight directions. And in order to speak a whole truth you have to be able to address all of them. Shakespeare knew this: you can only get intellectual so long and then you have to send Falstaff in or you get the rotten tomatoes. A well-rounded work of art, then, would have emotionality, sensuality, and so on. For instance, if you're going to play an instrument, it's best to be playing it from southwest or southeast because it needs the emotional influence. If you go to the west, your touch improves, your tactile intelligence wakes up. If you go towards the east your clarity wakes up, which means that the design would probably be less complex. If you're playing from the north the work is going to be very cold and mathematical. That's an idea that I've lived with all my life, and oddly enough, it's also a Chinese idea. Man once observed that the four directions exert an influence. It's hard in a world full of televisions and electrical gadgets to remember that. But that idea has been one of the major guiding tools of my life."

(Jana Lynne White, "The SpeakEasy Interview,"

CBC TV, March 22, 2000)

EMILY CARR

"I've been reading Emily Carr, who I love . . . I love her . . . It so helps to find a writer whose style I love and maybe it's because she's a painter but she . . . I've read a lot of great writers and I go 'Oh, this is a great writer,' but I don't love it. I can't explain it, it's just the way Emily Carr creates a sentence . . . they're like a songwriter's sentence, she's extremely gifted at condensing a lot into a very small space. She visually saturates her sentences in a way that's beyond compare to me. It's not so much that it's psychological . . . she just lets you see what she's seeing and lets the psychology take place."

VAN GOGH

"Of all the painters I felt most kindred to, I felt most touched by van Gogh. Van Gogh was impulsive. For him, art was like sex on the kitchen table."

(James Brooke, "For Joni Mitchell, Artist, Singing Was Not Enough," New York Times, August 22, 2000)

THE SECOND GREAT MILES DAVIS QUINTET

"That's my favorite pocket of Miles . . . *In a Silent Way* and *Nefertiti*, those two albums I played them a lot and that was my idea of the masterful music of that time period."

BEING BELOVED BY BLACK PEOPLE,
EVEN FORMER BLACK PANTHERS

"They're my best audience. The 'Joni Mitchell, she don't lie' school."

SOME SINGERS

"Ella Fitzgerald was mostly just a singer; Billie Holiday was more than a singer; Frank Sinatra was more than a singer. There were a lot that were Method actor singers. Etta James, you can't beat her read on 'At Last.' Céline Dion, with all her technique, she sings it plastic. But Etta, oh my God."

RECORDING WITH THE LONDON PHILHARMONIC

"Those sessions were so exciting in that the orchestra, as big as it was and it was one hundred ten pieces on some pieces—it was a huge orchestra breaking down to forty pieces—was sooo engaged . . . they were as engaged with the project as if they were a small band. They would pack into the playback room like little kids to listen back . . . they played especially on 'Both Sides, Now' and 'A Case of You' with great emotion. They didn't just read and pick up their paycheck and go home like a lot of orchestras in the past that I've played with. Because the department of music used to be so apartheid. Classical viewed itself as superior to pop. But this was a different generation, the orchestra was my age and younger, and they weren't snooty like when I was young and the orchestras played with me, it was like they were just doing it for the money and they were reading *The Wall Street Journal* behind their sheet music. Yeah . . . that orchestral version has such . . . there's a place where I get . . . have a surge of emotion and the whole orchestra goes with me."

TALKING

"I have to go to dinner in three hours, so we won't be able to marathon this conversation."

READER'S DIGEST

"I love *Reader's Digest*. I grew up on it, played 'Word Power.' In grade seven, I wrote a poem and there were two oversized words for an eleven-year-old in it. *Saffron* I got from my mother, and *equine* I got from 'Word Power.'"

(Mary Aikins, "Heart of a Prairie Girl," *Reader's Digest*, July 2005)

NEW RADICALS' SONG, 'YOU'VE GOT THE MUSIC IN YOU'

"The only thing I liked in a long time is the New Radicals' song. I love that song. That's the first song since I was a teenager that I rushed to the radio to turn up. I like the harmony, I like the passion in his voice. I love the song, you know, 'You got the music in you,' and I love the punk irreverence of it. Now, that's my kind of punky white boy."

(Q&A with David Wild, *Rolling Stone*, April 13, 2000)

METAPHOR

"I like metaphor. I've got Irish blood, and a love for metaphor seems to come along with the DNA." ("Black and Blond," Greg Tate, *Vibe*, December 1998)

BEING ALONE

"I like to just kind of free-agent it. I always was a loner. I like walking around in cities by myself. I can see things better. I mean, I've had some companions that I'm comfortable enough or compatible enough that I enjoy that, but often I just see better . . . I observe better when I'm on my own."

Acknowledgments

Thanks must go first of all to Joni Mitchell for her exquisite body of work, and for her willingness to talk with me about it. Steve Cline introduced me to Joni's music; Wayne Shorter took me to the bottom and top of it. Nikki Van De Car and my agent, David Dunton, came up with the idea for this book, and Dave then stewarded it through all the changes with grace and good humor. Wylie O'Sullivan of Free Press acquired the book with enthusiasm and edited it with acumen. Editorial assistants Donna Loffredo and Sydney Tanigawa were also instrumental in seeing the work into print.

Thanks to Jonifest and the JMDL for kicking it all off. Bernard Rouan, Leslie Mixon, David Hodes, and the Maidstone Museum for photos. Larry Klein and Luciana Souza for their expressive understanding of Joni's work. For other critical interviews: Michael Jensen and Graham Nash, Loudon Wainwright III, Bob Hinitt, Tony Simon, and Sharolyn Dickson. Special thanks to Pam and Tim Runkel for their hospitality and for facilitating my meetings and talks with Joni.

Philip Lopate and Sven Birkerts both provided significant criticism on the work-in-progress. Marc Neihof and Mitch Myers also read the manuscript in various stages.

My most heartfelt thanks to Les Irvin, who gave me inestimable help and support, and whose extraordinary maintenance of the official Joni Mitchell Web site makes research an easy task.

This book was started in the deep winter during a Vermont Studio Center residency and finished in the high summer at the Instituto Sacatar in Itaparica, Brazil. I am grateful to both foundations for fellowship support and beautiful working conditions.

Notes

Unless cited below or attributed to other sources in the text, quotations are from my original interviews. I would like to thank authors Karen O'Brien (*Joni Mitchell: Shadows and Light*) and Sheila Weller (*Girls Like Us*), whose research laid important groundwork for my understanding of Mitchell. Lloyd Whitesell's penetrating scholarly study (*The Music of Joni Mitchell*) informs the musical analysis throughout this book.

Introduction

3   *"I was roughly . . . existential transformation through* Blue*"*: Meghan Daum has laid claim to being the forty-nine millionth girl to experience the same thing through Mitchell's music. Meghan Daum, "The Missing Music," Speakeasy Magazine (speakeasymag.com), July 1, 2005.

4   *"But studies have shown . . . is the music that hits us deepest"*: The CBC producer Katrina Onstad drew this observation from the

work of Daniel Levitan. Katrina Onstad, "Joni's Blue period," http://www.cbc.ca/arts/music/joni.html, January 26, 2007.

8   *"bad metaphor for what . . . these poets were doing," "primary motive was aesthetic,":* Adam Kirsch, *The Wounded Surgeon: Confession and Transformation in Six American Poets* (New York: W. W. Norton and Co, 2005), p. x.

10   *"I'm not an uncheerful person . . . cheerful to face these themes":* Guy Garcia, "A Deeper Shade of Blue," *Time,* December 19, 1994.

11   *"it starts with a girl from . . . on La Brea in Los Angeles," "Do I want to know . . . There were a lot of us"* : J. Freedom du Lac, "Joni Mitchell's Blue 'River' Flows onto Holiday Playlists," *Washington Post,* December 21, 2006.

1. In the Manner of the Ancients

16   *"merely off on a lark . . . toward an unknown destination,"* Thomas Thompson, "Young American nomads abroad, two Californians at home in a cave in Matala, Crete": *Life,* July 19, 1968.

17   *"In the caves, last names had as little meaning as time":* Edward B. Fiske, "Students Are Living in Caves," *Nashua Telegraph,* August 30, 1967.

18   *"I was being isolated . . . in a crowd and moving freely," "The experiences I was having . . . I had to have other experiences":* Larry LeBlanc, "Joni Takes a Break," *Rolling Stone,* March 4, 1971.

19   *"penny yellow blonde with a vanilla voice":* Les Brown, "Joni Mitchell," *Rolling Stone,* July 6, 1968.

21   *"Is this the new phenomenon . . . running away from emotion?":* Thomas Thompson, "Young American nomads abroad, two Californians at home in a cave in Matala, Crete," *Life,* July 19, 1968.

21   *"Everybody was getting a little crazy . . . wearing little loincloths":* Ibid.

24   *"I was demanding of myself . . . very nerves of people's lives":* Joni

Mitchell: A Woman of Heart and Mind, American Masters series, PBS, 2003.

28   *"The* Confessions *is . . . core of a personal story"*: Patricia Hampl, *The Confessions: Saint Augustine.* (New York: Vintage: 1998), p. xvii.

29   *"great storyteller in . . . learned a lesson or two"*: Vic Garbarini, "Joni Mitchell Is a Nervy Broad," *Musician*, January 1983.

36   *"By Rousseau's age . . . important in their own right"*: J. M. Cohen, *The Confessions: Jean-Jacques Rousseau* (New York: Penguin Classics, 1953), p. 7.

37   *"My individual psychological . . . who they were worshiping"*: *Joni Mitchell: A Woman of Heart and Mind*, PBS.

38   *"The writing has been an . . . I want to say that in public?"*: Ibid.

45   *"some kind of therapeutic public purge or excretion"*: Sylvia Plath, *The Unabridged Journals of Sylvia Plath*, ed. Karen V. Kukil (New York: Anchor, 2000), p. 355.

45   *"more and more anguish and less and less poetry:"* Brett C. Miller, *Elizabeth Bishop: Life and the Memory of It* (Berkeley: University of California Press, 1993), p. 361.

2. Eyes on the Land and the Sky

51   *"Saskatchewan is in my veins . . . I'm a flatlander, period"*: *Canada A.M.*, television interview, CTV-TV, April 22, 2005.

52   *"One of the primary . . . geology followed by geography"*: Margaret Atwood, comment in Poetry Archive recording, www.poetry archive.org.

59   *"My years there were glorious, really . . . which usually constituted a grove of trees"*: Mary Aikins, "Heart of a Prairie Girl," *Reader's Digest*, July 2005.

60   *"The polio ward of St Paul's Hospital, Saskatoon . . . she was ready to go home"*: Jim Irvin, "Joni Mitchell," *Word*, March 2005.

61   *"Polio, in a way, germinated an inner life . . . mystical to come back from that disease"*: Ibid.

69 *"I gravitated to the best dance halls . . . someone saw me safely to the bus"*: William Ruhlman, "From Blue to Indigo," *Goldmine*, February 17, 1995.

72 *"That's one thing I resented . . . ruining its effectiveness and its value in your life"*: Robert Enright, "Words and Pictures: The Arts of Joni Mitchell," *Border Crossings*, February 2001.

76 *"I come from a wheat-farming community . . . they'll be happy to lop it off for you!"*: Camille Paglia, "The Trailblazer Interview," *Interview*, August 2005.

77 *"much of Joni's material was inspired by her impressions of life on the Prairies . . . and her love of the flat western landscape"*: "Rising Folksinger from Saskatoon Discusses Career," *Saskatoon StarPhoenix*, July 28, 1966.

78 *"How has the Canadian landscape . . . influenced your music?" "express a humble . . . they may know better," "My wife and I . . . land we're crossing," "sense of the . . . natural of dialogues"*: *Canadian Geographic*, http://www.canadiangeographic.ca/magazine/JF06/indepth/travel.asp.

81 *"I wanted to do all my own material . . . it was futile and it was silly, and I may as well quit"*: Dave Wilson, "An Interview with Joni Mitchell," *Broadside*, February 14, 1968.

82 *"I wrote ['Urge for Going'] in August . . . So I wrote 'Urge for Going' from that"*: Ibid.

82 *"He'd go into a club . . . opened up a whole circuit for me"*: Ian Mann, "Joni Mitchell," *ZigZag*, September 2, 1970.

84 *"I looked to her and . . . exerted an influence on me"*: Dave Di-Martino, "The Unfiltered Joni Mitchell," *Mojo*, August 1998.

88 *"I stepped outside of my little house . . . On Thursday the bear arrives"*: Liner Notes, *Shine*, Hear Music, 2007.

3. Art Songs

94 *"scholar Richard Sutherland has spoken of . . . from nineteenth-century*

French poet Charles Baudelaire": Eric Volmers, "Songbook: Folk fest artists find inspiration, subjects in literature," *Calgary Herald*, Thursday, July 24, 2008.

94   "*Critics who deny that legitimacy . . . while songs unite audiences in collective truths*": John Leland, "It's Only Rhyming Quatrains, but I Like It: Do Songs Succeed as Poetry," *The New York Times Magazine*, July 8, 2001.

97   "*This guy is so fucking bad . . . singing, then so can I!*" Les Irvin, "*A Conversation with John Uren*": JMDL.com, August 29, 2005.

100   "*Joni Mitchell . . . garbage and the flowers*": "Joni Mitchell," Les Brown, *Rolling Stone*, July 6, 1968.

100   "*I think I'm rather Cohen influenced . . . dramatic purposes*": Dave Wilson, "An Interview with Joni Mitchell," *Broadside*, February 14, 1968.

101   "*We Canadians are a bit more nosegay . . . strongly influenced by him*": Susan Gordon Lydon, "In Her House, Love," *New York Times*, April 20, 1969.

101   "The musicologist Lloyd Whitesell has analyzed Mitchell's highly wrought attention to poetic construction": *The Music of Joni Mitchell* (New York: Oxford University Press, 2008), pp. 17–19.

104   "*Like the Talmud says, there's good wine in every generation*": Leonard Cohen in interview with Robert Sward, 1984, http://www.leonardcohenfiles.com/sward.html.

105   "*held a mirror up . . . depth of my experiences*": Stewart Brand, "The Education of Joni Mitchell," *Co-Evolution Quarterly*, June 1976.

106   "*But we have a special . . . we used to make love to*": Leonard Cohen, http://www.leonardcohenfiles.com/sward.html.

106   "*Americans seem to like . . . That's generally the pattern*": Radio interview for *Morning Becomes Eclectic*, KCRW-FM, September 12, 1994.

107   "*You know, in standard tuning . . . to get away from that*":

"Words and Music—Joni Mitchell and Morrissey," a promotional interview for Reprise Records, October 18, 1996.

108   *"Immediately, it gave . . . would have gone to the piano"*: Robert Hilburn, "An Art Born of Pain, an Artist in Happy Exile," *Los Angeles Times*, September 05, 2004.

108   *"Her open tunings . . . entirely new ways of feeling in music"*: This analysis is partly drawn from Susan Lacy's comments. Susan Lacy, "Web Interview with Susan Lacy," www.pbs.org/wnet/americanmasters/database/mitchell_j_interview.html>, April 2003.

114   *"In portraying herself so starkly, she has risked the ridiculous to achieve the sublime"*: Timothy Crouse, "Blue," *Rolling Stone*, August 5, 1971.

114   *"I would have to . . . a lyrical point of view"*: Steven Daly, "Rock and Roll," *Rolling Stone*, October 29, 1998.

114   *"The expression of her extraordinary . . . who can come even near"*: Annie Lennox, Liner Notes to *A Tribute to Joni Mitchell*, Nonesuch, 2007.

115   *"I suspect this will be the most disliked . . . having to make a decision between the two"*: Dan Heckman, "Joni Mitchell at a Crossroads," *New York Times*, August 8, 1971.

4. Singing the Blues Makes You Bluer

119   *"When Barry Lopez . . . and you never feel alone"*: Bob Shacochis, lecture at Bennington Writing Seminars, January 2008 residency.

121   *"many of Mrs. Sexton's . . . nor the reader's either"*: *Times Literary Supplement*, May 18, 1967.

122   *"The obligation to confess . . . at the price of a kind of liberation"*: Michel Foucault, *The History of Sexuality*, p. 60.

123   *"For me the private act . . . one inexpensive package"*: Stephen Fry, *The Ode Less Travelled: Unlocking the Poet Within* (New York: Gotham Books, 2005), p. xii.

130   *"almost like a monastery . . . corrective shoe"*: Marci McDonald, "Joni Mitchell Emerges from her Retreat," *Toronto Star*, February 9, 1974.

143   *"Like its lyrics, For the Roses' music . . . variable music evincing highly personal feeling"*: This analysis is informed by Randall Davis's insightful review of *For the Roses*. Randall Davis, "Musical Notes," *Arcadia Tribune*, December 14, 1972.

144   *"One day about a year . . . my inner happiness was still intact"*: Vic Garbarini, "Joni Mitchell Is a Nervy Broad," *Musician*, January 1983.

5. Beyond Personal Songwriting

151   *"In 1972, it looked as . . . the movement disintegrated"*: Stephen Holden, "Singer-Songwriters Spin Their Tales," *New York Times*, April 3, 1988.

154   *"Without naming names . . . the better musician you will be"*: David Hoekstra, http://blogs.suntimes.com/hoekstra/2008/07/billy_joel.html.

154   *"I thought, You'd better . . . the source of her celebrity"*: Alice Echols, "Thirty Years with a Portable Lover," *Los Angeles Weekly*, November 25, 1994.

155   *"The Rolling Stones . . . his career is the opposite," "James himself perpetuates . . . aims at their solution"*: Ben Gerson, "Review: Mud Slide Slim & The Blue Horizon," *Rolling Stone*, June 24, 1971.

158   *"I don't want to be vulnerable . . . absorb some of the loneliness"*: "Joni Mitchell Emerges from her Retreat," Marci McDonald, *Toronto Star*, February 9, 1974.

161   *"Joni Mitchell's unique . . . in the lyrics themselves"*: Brad Mehldau, Liner Notes to *A Tribute To Joni Mitchell*, Nonesuch Records, 2007.

162   *"On Court and Spark . . . the possessiveness of romantic idealism"*: I'm drawing here on Stephen Holden's fine review of

the recording. Stephen Holden, "Court and Spark," *Zoo World*, March 14, 1974.

166   *"Joni Mitchell's lyrics . . . especially for women"*: Robert Christgau, "For the Roses," *Newsday*, January 1973.

6. The Breadth of Extremities

170   *"Antique pieces crowd tables, mantels, and shelves . . . making the crust for a rhubarb pie"*: "Joni Mitchell," *Rolling Stone*, May 17, 1969.

177   *"As the scholar Daniel Sonenberg has noted"*: Sonenberg, " 'Who in the World She Might Be': A Contextual and Stylistic Approach to the Early Music of Joni Mitchell" (D.M.A. diss., City University of New York, 2003), pp. 83–104.

178   *"You could write with your feelings . . . human emotions was material enough"*: Rick Moody, "On the Granite Steps of the Madhouse with Shaven Heads," in *The Poem That Changed America: "Howl" Fifty Years Later*, ed. Jason Shinder (New York: Farrar, Straus and Giroux, 2006), p. 63.

179   *"a breakthrough . . . lay it out on the page"*: Allen Ginsberg, "Revolutionary Poetics," Lecture at Naropa University, July 4, 1989.

179   *"brought a terrible . . . hairsbreadth forward in the process"*: M. L. Rosenthal, "Review of *Howl and Other Poems*," *The Nation*, February 23, 1957.

179   *"distant, symbol-ridden, and willfully difficult . . . I was reciting what I no longer felt,"* *"On 'Skunk Hour' "*: Robert Lowell, *Collected Prose*, ed. Robert Giroux (New York: Farrar, Straus and Giroux, 1987).

180   *"came out of the wilderness and just naturally fell in with the Beat scene . . . On the Road, Dean Moriarty, this made perfect sense to me"*: Cameron Crowe, Liner Notes to *Biograph*, 1985, p. 5.

181 *"a very rational and classical approach to Buddhism . . . 'Go sit, weeks and weeks and weeks, ten hours a day,'"* Peter Barry Chowka, "This is Allen Ginsberg?" *New Age Journal*, April 1976.

181 *"exemplified in William Carlos Williams's brief poems . . . resolve to dream no more":* Ibid.

183 *"A hundred bucks' worth of Valiums are delivered to the Niagara Hilton like so much Chicken Delight":* Sam Shepard, *Rolling Thunder Logbook* (New York: Da Capo Press, 2004), p. 114.

183 *"More talk of shooting concerts":* Ibid., p. 132.

184 *"They asked me how I wanted to be paid . . . because everybody was strung out on cocaine":* Mary Aikins, "Heart of a Prairie Girl," *Reader's Digest*, July 2005.

184 *"Joni Mitchell was habitually writing lyrics . . . image of Errol Flynn in a sarong":* Roger McGuinn, "Roadie Report 31—'The Rolling Thunder Revue,'" http://rogermcguinn.blogspot. com/2007/11/roadie-report-31-rolling-thunder-revue.html.

185 *"Mitchell's greatest third-person song . . . with a putative erotic value":* Stephen Holden, "Madam Joni Almost Pulls It Off," *Village Voice*, December 19, 1977.

185 *"If some people had their way . . . I got rid of that one":* David Wild, "A Conversation with Joni Mitchell," *Rolling Stone*, May 30, 1991.

199 *"An old, funky lighthouse-keeping place on the beach," "It was a relief . . . fall in with people and enjoy ordinary civilian status":* Doug Fischer, "The Trouble She's Seen," *Ottawa Citizen*, October 8, 2006.

201 *"The effect of this harmonic design . . . three lines to come gently tumbling out in perfect acoustic symmetry":* Tom Manoff, *Music: A Living Language* (New York: W. W. Norton and Co, 1982).

Index

Note: Music titles are by Joni Mitchell unless otherwise noted.

About the Author

Michelle Mercer, a regular contributor to National Public Radio, is the author of the critically acclaimed biography *Footprints: The Life and Work of Wayne Shorter.* Her articles have appeared in *The New York Times*, *The Village Voice*, *DownBeat*, and elsewhere. She lives in Colorado and Bahia, Brazil.